*Byron Anderson, MA, MLIS*
*Paul T. Webb, MA, MLIS*
*Editors*

# New Directions
# in Reference

*New Directions in Reference* has been co-published simultaneously as *The Reference Librarian*, Number 93 2006.

*Pre-publication*
*REVIEWS,*
*COMMENTARIES,*
*EVALUATIONS . . .*

"**E**XCELLENT. . . . Chronicles how a diverse cross-section of libraries are embracing change and incorporating technological developments into their reference services. EACH CHAPTER DISCUSSES NEW IDEAS, CHALLENGES, AND DIRECTIONS FOR REFERENCE SERVICES."

**Tim Daniels, MLIS**
*Learning Commons Coordinator*
*and Digital Technologies Librarian*
*Georgia State University Library*

The Haworth Information Press®
An Imprint of The Haworth Press, Inc.

# New Directions
# in Reference

*New Directions in Reference* has been co-published simultaneously as *The Reference Librarian*, Number 93 2006.

*New Directions in Reference,* edited by Byron Anderson, MA, MLIS, and Paul T. Webb, MA, MLIS (No. 93, 2006). *"An interesting collection. . . . I was especially intrigued by Harry Meserve's insider's evaluation of San José's merger of public and university library services, and Anderson's activist call for librarians to fight aspects of the Digital Millennium Copyright Act." (Andrew B. Werthheimer, PhD, Assistant Professor, Library & Information Science Program, University of Hawaii at Manoa)*

*The Reference Collection: From the Shelf to the Web,* edited by William J. Frost (No. 91/92, 2005). *An essential guide to collection development for electronic materials in academic and public libraries.*

*Relationships Between Teaching Faculty and Teaching Librarians,* edited by Susan B. Kraat (No. 89/90, 2005). *Documents the efforts of teaching librarians to establish effective communication with teaching faculty.*

*Research, Reference Service, and Resources for the Study of Africa,* edited by Deborah M. LaFond and Gretchen Walsh (No. 87/88, 2004). *Examines reference services in terms of Africa and libraries in both the United States and Africa.*

*Animals Are the Issue: Library Resources on Animal Issues,* edited by John M. Kistler, MLS, MDiv (No. 86, 2004). *Contains listings of written and electronic resources that focus on the ethics of animal treatment and use.*

*Digital versus Non-Digital Reference: Ask a Librarian Online and Offline,* edited by Jessamyn West, MLib (No. 85, 2004). *A librarian's guide to commercial Ask A Librarian (AskA) and tutorial services and how they compare to traditional library services.*

*Cooperative Reference: Social Interaction in the Workplace,* edited by Celia Hales Mabry, PhD (No. 83/84, 2003). *This informative volume focuses on effective social interactions between library co-workers, presenting perspectives, firsthand accounts, and advice from experienced and successful reference librarians.*

*Outreach Services in Academic and Special Libraries,* edited by Paul Kelsey, MLIS, and Sigrid Kelsey, MLIS (No. 82, 2003). *Presents an array of models and case studies for creating and implementing outreach services in academic and special library settings.*

*Managing the Twenty-First Century Reference Department: Challenges and Prospects,* edited by Kwasi Sarkodie-Mensah, PhD (No. 81, 2003). *An up-to-date guide on managing and maintaining a reference department in the twenty-first century.*

*Digital Reference Services,* edited by Bill Katz, PhD (No. 79/80, 2002/2003). *A clear and concise book explaining developments in electronic technology for reference services and their implications for reference librarians.*

*The Image and Role of the Librarian,* edited by Wendi Arant, MLS, and Candace R. Benefiel, MA, MLIS (No. 78, 2002). *A unique and insightful examination of how librarians are perceived–and how they perceive themselves.*

*Distance Learning: Information Access and Services for Virtual Users,* edited by Hemalata Iyer, PhD (No. 77, 2002). *Addresses the challenge of providing Web-based library instructional materials in a time of ever-changing technologies.*

***Helping the Difficult Library Patron: New Approaches to Examining and Resolving a Long-Standing and Ongoing Problem,*** edited by Kwasi Sarkodie-Mensah, PhD (No. 75/76, 2002). *"Finally! A book that fills in the information cracks not covered in library school about the ubiquitous problem patron. Required reading for public service librarians." (Cheryl LaGuardia, MLS, Head of Instructional Services for the Harvard College Library, Cambridge, Massachusetts)*

***Evolution in Reference and Information Services: The Impact of the Internet,*** edited by Di Su, MLS (No. 74, 2001). *Helps you make the most of the changes brought to the profession by the Internet.*

***Doing the Work of Reference: Practical Tips for Excelling as a Reference Librarian,*** edited by Celia Hales Mabry, PhD (No. 72 and 73, 2001). *"An excellent handbook for reference librarians who wish to move from novice to expert. Topical coverage is extensive and is presented by the best guides possible: practicing reference librarians." (Rebecca Watson-Boone, PhD, President, Center for the Study of Information Professionals, Inc.)*

***New Technologies and Reference Services,*** edited by Bill Katz, PhD (No. 71, 2000). *This important book explores developing trends in publishing, information literacy in the reference environment, reference provision in adult basic and community education, searching sessions, outreach programs, locating moving image materials for multimedia development, and much more.*

***Reference Services for the Adult Learner: Challenging Issues for the Traditional and Technological Era,*** edited by Kwasi Sarkodie-Mensah, PhD (No. 69/70, 2000). *Containing research from librarians and adult learners from the United States, Canada, and Australia, this comprehensive guide offers you strategies for teaching adult patrons that will enable them to properly use and easily locate all of the materials in your library.*

***Library Outreach, Partnerships, and Distance Education: Reference Librarians at the Gateway,*** edited by Wendi Arant and Pixey Anne Mosley (No. 67/68, 1999). *Focuses on community outreach in libraries toward a broader public by extending services based on recent developments in information technology.*

***From Past-Present to Future-Perfect: A Tribute to Charles A. Bunge and the Challenges of Contemporary Reference Service,*** edited by Chris D. Ferguson, PhD (No. 66, 1999). *Explore reprints of selected articles by Charles Bunge, bibliographies of his published work, and original articles that draw on Bunge's values and ideas in assessing the present and shaping the future of reference service.*

***Reference Services and Media,*** edited by Martha Merrill, PhD (No. 65, 1999). *Gives you valuable information about various aspects of reference services and media, including changes, planning issues, and the use and impact of new technologies.*

***Coming of Age in Reference Services: A Case History of the Washington State University Libraries,*** edited by Christy Zlatos, MSLS (No. 64, 1999). *A celebration of the perseverance, ingenuity, and talent of the librarians who have served, past and present, at the Holland Library reference desk.*

***Document Delivery Services: Contrasting Views,*** edited by Robin Kinder, MLS (No. 63, 1999). *Reviews the planning and process of implementing document delivery in four university libraries–Miami University, University of Colorado at Denver, University of Montana at Missoula, and Purdue University Libraries.*

***The Holocaust: Memories, Research, Reference,*** edited by Robert Hauptman, PhD, and Susan Hubbs Motin (No. 61/62, 1998). *"A wonderful resource for reference librarians, students, and teachers . . . on how to present this painful, historical event." (Ephraim Kaye, PhD, The International School for Holocaust Studies, Yad Vashem, Jerusalem)*

***Electronic Resources: Use and User Behavior,*** edited by Hemalata Iyer, PhD (No. 60, 1998). *Covers electronic resources and their use in libraries, with emphasis on the Internet and the Geographic Information Systems (GIS).*

# New Directions in Reference

Byron Anderson, MA, MLIS
Paul T. Webb, MA, MLIS
Editors

*New Directions in Reference* has been co-published simultaneously as *The Reference Librarian*, Number 93 2006.

The Haworth Information Press®
An Imprint of The Haworth Press, Inc.

New York • London • Victoria (AU)
www.HaworthPress.com

Published by

The Haworth Information Press®, 10 Alice Street, Binghamton, NY 13904-1580 USA

The Haworth Information Press® is an imprint of The Haworth Press, Inc., 10 Alice Street, Binghamton, NY 13904-1580 USA.

*New Directions in Reference* has been co-published simultaneously as *The Reference Librarian*™, Number 93 2006.

The development, preparation, and publication of this work has been undertaken with great care. However, the publisher, employees, editors, and agents of The Haworth Press and all imprints of The Haworth Press, Inc., including The Haworth Medical Press® and Pharmaceutical Products Press®, are not responsible for any errors contained herein or for consequences that may ensue from use of materials or information contained in this work. With regard to case studies, identities and circumstances of individuals discussed herein have been changed to protect confidentiality. Any resemblance to actual persons, living or dead, is entirely coincidental.

The Haworth Press is committed to the dissemination of ideas and information according to the highest standards of intellectual freedom and the free exchange of ideas. Statements made and opinions expressed in this publication do not necessarily reflect the views of the Publisher, Directors, management, or staff of The Haworth Press, Inc., or an endorsement by them.

Cover design by Wendy Arakawa.

**Library of Congress Cataloging-in-Publication Data**

New directions in reference / Byron Anderson, Paul T. Webb, editors.
      p. cm.
      "Co-published simultaneously as The reference librarian, number 93, 2006."
      Includes bibliographical references and index.
      ISBN-13: 978-0-7890-3088-7 (alk. paper)
      ISBN-10: 0-7890-3088-8 (alk. paper)
      ISBN-13: 978-0-7890-3089-4 (pbk. : alk. paper)
      ISBN-10: 0-7890-3089-6 (pbk. : alk. paper)
      1. Electronic reference services (Libraries) 2. Internet in library reference services. 3. Reference services (Libraries)–Technological innovations. 4. Reference librarians–Effect of technological innovations on. 5. Reference services (Libraries)–United States. I. Anderson, Byron. II. Webb, Paul T. III. Reference librarian.

Z711.45.N49 2006
025.5'2–dc22
                                        2005019482

# Indexing, Abstracting & Website/Internet Coverage

This section provides you with a list of major indexing & abstracting services and other tools for bibliographic access. That is to say, each service began covering this periodical during the year noted in the right column. Most Websites which are listed below have indicated that they will either post, disseminate, compile, archive, cite or alert their own Website users with research-based content from this work. (This list is as current as the copyright date of this publication.)

(continued)

(continued)

*Special bibliographic notes related to special journal issues (separates) and indexing/abstracting:*

- indexing/abstracting services in this list will also cover material in any "separate" that is co-published simultaneously with Haworth's special thematic journal issue or DocuSerial. Indexing/abstracting usually covers material at the article/chapter level.
- monographic co-editions are intended for either non-subscribers or libraries which intend to purchase a second copy for their circulating collections.
- monographic co-editions are reported to all jobbers/wholesalers/approval plans. The source journal is listed as the "series" to assist the prevention of duplicate purchasing in the same manner utilized for books-in-series.
- to facilitate user/access services all indexing/abstracting services are encouraged to utilize the co-indexing entry note indicated at the bottom of the first page of each article/chapter/contribution.
- this is intended to assist a library user of any reference tool (whether print, electronic, online, or CD-ROM) to locate the monographic version if the library has purchased this version but not a subscription to the source journal.
- individual articles/chapters in any Haworth publication are also available through the Haworth Document Delivery Service (HDDS).

# New Directions
# in Reference

## CONTENTS

ISSUES IN LIBRARY SERVICES

## ABOUT THE EDITORS

**Byron Anderson, MA, MLIS,** is Professor and Head of Reference at the University Libraries, Northern Illinois University, DeKalb, Illinois. He received his MA in History and MLIS in Library and Information Science from the University of Wisconsin-Milwaukee. His research and publications have focused on issues surrounding technology's effect on librarianship as a profession, intellectual freedom, and the independent press. His column, Electronic Roundup, regularly appears in the journal, *Behavioral & Social Sciences Librarian.* He is Compiler/Editor of *Alternative Publishers of Books in North America,* now in its 5th edition (2002) from CRISES Press. He has been on the Editorial Board of *The Reference Librarian* since 1992.

**Paul T. Webb, MA, MLIS,** is Assistant Professor and Social Sciences and Humanities Librarian at the University Libraries, Northern Illinois University, DeKalb, Illinois. He serves as the subject bibliographer for Political Science, Philosophy & Religion, Economics, and Foreign Languages & Literatures. Professor Webb graduated from Southern Illinois University-Carbondale with a BA and MA in History, and received his MS in Library Science from the University of Illinois at Urbana-Champaign. Professor Webb's research interests include citation studies, free electronic journals, and Cold War historiography.

# IN MEMORIAM

## William Katz

Dr. William (Bill) Katz passed away on September 12, 2004. Dr. Katz was Editor of the Haworth journals *The Acquisitions Librarian* and *The Reference Librarian* as well as *Magazines for Libraries*, *RQ* (the journal of the Reference and Adult Services Division of the American Library Association), and the "Magazines" column in *Library Journal.* In addition to his contributions to library science as an author and editor, he was a much-beloved professor in the School of Information Science and Policy at the State University of New York at Albany and a mentor to many of his former students in their professional lives. His association with The Haworth Press began in 1980 and lasted more than two decades. His steady hand, friendly guidance, and steadfast leadership will be missed by all of us at *The Acquisitions Librarian*, *The Reference Librarian*, and The Haworth Press.

# Introduction

Byron Anderson
Paul T. Webb

Librarians work in an environment of constant change driven largely by technology, but are also affected by budget restraints, inflationary costs, and rising user expectations. The articles here demonstrate that changes are so sweeping as to give new directions to reference services. At the same time, some things never change but need to be re-applied, especially as libraries enter into virtual reference services, as Buckley's article, "Golden Rule Reference" reminds us.

Change is not new to libraries. Rather, the pace of change has broadened influencing everything in its path. The articles discuss a wide range of changes and how these affect libraries, librarians, and patrons. For example, Burk clearly indicates that interlibrary loan is moving toward a self-service model and Burnette and Dorsch's report shows new ground gained in the use of Personal Digital Assistants in medical libraries. Can this technology be far off from usage in public and academic libraries? And Anderson explains how recent copyright acts are undermining the foundations of libraries, and why librarians must step up their efforts in protecting intellectual freedom.

The lines that have traditionally existed between library departments are becoming blurred. Lines between general reference and specialized reference are blurring as Duffy points out in "Current Issues in Music Reference." Even the distinct lines between public and academic libraries have been merged as shown by Merserve's "Evolving Reference, Changing Culture."

[Haworth co-indexing entry note]: "Introduction." Anderson, Byron, and Paul T. Webb. Co-published simultaneously in *The Reference Librarian* (The Haworth Information Press, an imprint of The Haworth Press, Inc.) No. 93, 2006, pp. 1-2; and: *New Directions in Reference* (ed: Byron Anderson, and Paul T. Webb) The Haworth Information Press, an imprint of The Haworth Press, Inc., 2006, pp. 1-2. Single or multiple copies of this article are available for a fee from The Haworth Document Delivery Service [1-800-HAWORTH, 9:00 a.m. - 5:00 p.m. (EST). E-mail address: docdelivery@haworthpress.com].

Available online at http://www.haworthpress.com/web/REF
doi:10.1300/J120v45n93_01

Within the broad sweep of change affecting libraries, there is good news. In a well-documented story, Hathaway is able to be upbeat about the future of accessibility of government information. Lindbloom et al. explore virtual reference as a new career opportunity for librarians. VandeCreek shows that new service areas can open when based on user feedback.

The onus of change is clearly on reference librarians who must broaden their scope of knowledge in providing their services. The articles encompass all types of libraries–public, academic, special and virtual. Even Standerfer's "Reference Services in Rural Libraries" is able to demonstrate broad changes affecting small and rural libraries. Reading about the experiences of librarians in types of libraries different from the one you're currently working in, can be informative. Ideas presented in these articles may well jog your brain and give you something to think about.

General conclusions can be drawn from the articles. Change has set new directions for reference services. This will continue indefinitely and may increase to a greater extent than experienced to date. For example, a new technology, Radio Frequency Identification tags, used for tracking consumer products, is being experimented with in libraries in locating library materials, speeding up checkout, and deterring thefts. There's also the issue of patron confidentiality in the use of this these microchips. There are many more examples. No library is exempt from the changes now occurring. Librarians will continue into the foreseeable future to adjust to new technology, budget constraints, inflationary costs, and rising user expectations.

# NEW ROLES FOR LIBRARIANS

# Virtual Reference:
# A Reference Question
# Is a Reference Question . . .
# Or Is Virtual Reference a New Reality?
# New Career Opportunities for Librarians

Mary-Carol Lindbloom
Anna Yackle
Skip Burhans
Tom Peters
Lori Bell

Mary-Carol Lindbloom is Library Development Consultant, Alliance Library System, 515 York Street, Quincy, IL 62301 (E-mail: mclindbloom@AllianceLibrarySystem. com). Anna Yackle is Consultant, North Suburban Library System, 200 West Dundee Road, Wheeling, IL 60090 (E-mail: ayackle@nsls.info). Skip Burhans was Project Coordinator, MyWebLibrarian.com (E-mail: sburnhans@abac.com). Tom Peters is founder of TAP Information Services, 1000 S.W. 23rd Street, Blue Springs, MO 64015 (E-mail: tapinformation@yahoo.com). Lori Bell is Director, Mid-Illinois Talking Book Center, Alliance Library System, 600 High Point Lane, East Peoria, IL 61611 (E-mail: lbell@AllianceLibrarySystem.com).

[Haworth co-indexing entry note]: "Virtual Reference: A Reference Question Is a Reference Question . . . Or Is Virtual Reference a New Reality? New Career Opportunities for Librarians." Lindbloom et al. Co-published simultaneously in *The Reference Librarian* (The Haworth Information Press, an imprint of The Haworth Press, Inc.) No. 93, 2006, pp. 3-22; and: *New Directions in Reference* (ed: Byron Anderson, and Paul T. Webb) The Haworth Information Press, an imprint of The Haworth Press, Inc., 2006, pp. 3-22. Single or multiple copies of this article are available for a fee from The Haworth Document Delivery Service [1-800-HAWORTH, 9:00 a.m. - 5:00 p.m. (EST). E-mail address: docdelivery@haworthpress.com].

Available online at http://www.haworthpress.com/web/REF
© 2006 by The Haworth Press, Inc. All rights reserved.
doi:10.1300/J120v45n93_02

**SUMMARY.** Explores virtual reference as a new career opportunity for librarians. Asks if this is a good, long career path, or if it will careen virtual reference librarians off into the slough of despond. The skills needed for the traditional reference librarian are compared to those needed by the virtual reference librarian; the challenges and advantages of working virtual versus traditional reference are identified; the types of questions and resources used in providing virtual reference service are discussed; and the types of interaction with the patrons are explored. The skills needed to manage and evaluate virtual reference services are also articulated. *[Article copies available for a fee from The Haworth Document Delivery Service: 1-800-HAWORTH. E-mail address: <docdelivery@haworthpress.com> Website: <http://www.HaworthPress.com> © 2006 by The Haworth Press, Inc. All rights reserved.]*

**KEYWORDS.** Virtual reference, career opportunities, skills transfer, cooperative reference, commercial reference, working from home, reference interview

In gathering information for this article, from September 1 to September 15, 2003, a brief, informal, online survey was conducted of subscribers of two virtual reference electronic mailing lists: Dig_Ref from The Virtual Reference Desk, http://www.vrd.org, and live reference, http://groups.yahoo.com/group/livereference. The survey instrument is included as an appendix at the end of this article. Throughout the article, the authors also used their shared experiences to discuss new career opportunities in virtual reference. The authors' collective experiences in virtual reference include: contract work for a VR vendor; contract work for coordination of a virtual reference project; management of a public library virtual reference service; management of an academic virtual reference service; management of a multi-type virtual reference service; work at the VR desk for all types of libraries; and evaluation of online reference services.

## A BRIEF HISTORY OF VIRTUAL (REFERENCE) TIME

Until four years ago, if you wanted a career in reference librarianship, the qualifications and duties of the job included the following: an extensive knowledge of print and electronic reference resources; the ability to provide in-person instruction on these resources one-on-one and for groups; and the necessity to work a certain number of hours per week at a traditional reference desk, assisting patrons in-person, via telephone, and sometimes even by electronic mail. The hours worked were spent in a physical library building or space and might have included some evening and weekend hours–the dreaded weekend rotation. Even if a multitude of electronic resources were available, the main reference resource was the print reference collection, and the reference desk was the service focal point. With the new millennium came the implementation of virtual reference services in all types of libraries.

## *DEFINITIONS*

This latest subspecies of reference services does not yet have an agreed upon name, and has been labeled, defined, and described many ways: Virtual; Real-time; Synchronous; Chat; Instant Messaging; Electronic; Digital; Online. Electronic, digital, and online forms of reference have been around for many years, in the form of e-mail reference and library Web sites that contain reference forms for a user to complete and send (usually to an e-mail account). The present article employs the phrase "virtual reference" and the authors define it as a synchronous electronic form of communication between librarian and user, which includes the capability of sending information in electronic form (text and images) and contains one or more of the following components: text chat, voice, and video. Lipow (2002) refers to a "virtual reference librarian" as "a librarian who provides point-of-need live, interactive question-handling using chat and voice software that enable synchronous communication with a distant client." Not everyone, however, is comfortable with the phrase "virtual reference." For example, Pace (2003) remarks, "The very notion of virtuality–something less than real–diminishes the reality of hard work, new paradigms, and the shifting set of skills required to do the job of librarianship."

## *MODELS FOR SERVICE PROVISION*

Along with the software development that made virtual reference possible, several organizational models for service provision emerged. Librarians working in traditional libraries learned the skills to offer virtual reference services; several companies including LSSI, recently acquired by Tutor.com, and 24/7 hired librarians to provide virtual reference services from their homes on a contract basis. A few librarians went into business for themselves to offer these services to individual clients or libraries. Some VR services mix and match the basic models to come up with a hybrid. For example, KnowItNow, the VR service of CLEVNET, relies on Tutor.com to contract VR librarians to answer 24 percent of all questions fielded (Kenney 2003). Librarians working in organizations that incorporated VR into their umbrella of reference services discovered very quickly that they had to become comfortable "text chatting" with unseen patrons and using electronic and Internet resources as the main sources of information. Traditional reference librarians who might have been comfortable using computers and performing online database searches still had to become "at ease" with "text chatting." If a librarian wanted to work an additional job as a virtual reference librarian on a contractual basis, willingness to work evenings, weekends and the wee hours was a prerequisite.

## *SKILL SET:*
## *TRADITIONAL versus VIRTUAL*

Is virtual reference service a new reality? One librarian responding to the survey stated, "The new reality for me is that a patron is a patron is a patron." Virtual reference librarianship is dependent upon many of the skills required of conventional reference librarianship, including: the ability to conduct an effective reference interview, to communicate effectively, and to cheerfully assist the user in selecting and using the best resources. If a VR librarian does not have those basic skills, one librarian in the survey stated, "no matter how good the technology is, it won't make up for an ineffective reference librarian." Several librarians stated they like the adrenalin rush of virtual work and that the question seems more immediate than at a traditional reference desk. Other librarians responding to the survey stated that librarians should not throw away traditional reference skills in doing virtual reference–traditional reference skills are the cornerstone for providing reference in any context or environment. So what is different about the virtual environment? The new reality is that the librarian must also have an additional set of technology skills and knowledge to effectively provide virtual reference service. Pace (2003) writes, "The virtual reference desk is a perfect example of professional requirements and expectations changing right in front of us. . . ."

Although most librarians working in the 21st century library need to be comfortable using a computer, the Internet, and online databases, virtual reference requires the librarian to have a more extensive knowledge of Internet and online resources. They need to be knowledgeable about Internet search engines and must keep up-to-date. VR librarians need to be able to perform quick and efficient searches of electronic resources. They need to be flexible, able to multi-task and handle more than one session at a time, and quickly establish a rapport in an electronic environment. It is not uncommon for in-house librarians to work with multiple users, getting one started using resources, while helping another. In the virtual environment, however, a librarian cannot rely on body kinesics and has the added challenge of keeping lines of communication going while troubleshooting potential problems with a PC, Internet connection, and VR software.

## THE REFERENCE INTERVIEW

Indeed, the reference interview in the virtual world is somewhat similar but at the same time very different than the traditional interview. Elias and Merrill (2003) noted, "We all had to find a balance between being welcoming and being efficient when chatting with patrons." The premise is that a patron has a need for information and is either seeking assistance from a librarian to obtain that information, or instruction in how to obtain it. The first difference is that in a text-chat environment, the librarian and patron cannot see one another–the interaction lacks non-verbal clues and even voice clues, unless they are using a program with audio. Most current virtual reference programs rely heavily on text chat, which may be a short-lived phenomenon. If reliable voice-over-IP has arrived, can reliable video-over-IP be far behind? A virtual reference librarian must be comfortable using "text chat," the dos and don'ts of communication on the Internet, and Internet chat protocols and netiquette. Typing skills and the ability to type quickly and error-free suddenly become important. In fact, typing quickly is more important than accuracy (except for keywords), and this alone can be difficult for librarians to embrace. The ability to convey "friendliness" and a helpful attitude, all through text chat, are other skills needed for a successful online reference interview. Often a good, sufficient answer to a reference question is constructed through a series of brief chat responses, rather than one long answer after a considerable period of research. Some virtual reference librarians use emoticons to convey friendliness, and a few may employ "chat lingo." In any case, throughout the virtual reference interview, the librarian is dependent upon a computer, an Internet connection, and the VR software for a satisfactory reference session. There are not as many inherent environmental barriers in a face-to-face reference session. One librarian who preferred the traditional environment said she did not like to multi-task; when assisting a patron, she preferred to give that patron all of her attention.

Those who preferred the virtual environment said it forced them to remain up-to-date on online resources and maintain their technology skills. Several librarians stated they preferred VR because it was new and exciting. One librarian said that she felt she could do more searching effectively without the patron breathing down her neck; another one said she found VR patrons are more impatient. Another preferred VR because "there are no physical boundaries."

## *VIRTUAL REFERENCE CUSTOMERS AND ONLINE COMMUNICATION*

Many virtual reference customers may not use the traditional library on a regular basis. Sloan (2003) found supporting data during his evaluation of the MyWebLibrarian service. Users had been asked to identify the sources of information they use the most frequently. When 71.41 percent of respondents identified "the Internet/Web" as their first choice, Sloan suggested, "MWL is reaching an audience that does not readily think of libraries as a source of information. If that is the case, then virtual reference services might be considered to be a way for libraries to reach users who do not frequent the physical library." He goes on to remark that "on the other hand, it is interesting to note that one out of five respondents think of libraries first as a source of information, which would suggest that perhaps some users of the physical library also embrace virtual library resources and services."

Certainly, by offering VR services, a library can reach out to new users. The majority of users of both public and academic virtual reference services are students, and they are grateful for the assistance that they receive. One of the problems with the VR environment is that it is easier for patrons to be rude and abusive to librarians. One surveyed librarian compared a problem patron to someone making prank phone calls. The types of problem patrons encountered in the virtual arena are somewhat different than those experienced in the physical one. In the physical environment, a problem patron may abuse a variety of departments before s/he is stopped. Circulation may bear the brunt of patrons angry over fines or borrower's card requirements. The reference department may field complaints about Internet and other public-use policies, often must maintain order in the reading area, and deal with sleeping patrons. In-house problem patrons can be dangerous, perhaps even deadly, and an immediate security risk to librarians, other patrons, and library equipment and materials. In the virtual environment, abuse may not be immediately life-threatening, but is still unpleasant, demeaning, and may occur for a variety of reasons: the patron is frustrated, s/he may not believe there is a human at the other end of the computer, they may be researching while intoxicated, or there may just be a communication problem. Libraries and cooperative services need to have written policies on how to handle problem behavior in the virtual environment to ensure consistency of responses.

MyWebLibrarian.com, launched in April 2003 without a written policy, received a string of abusive users within the first few days. Meanwhile, a group of librarians within the Illinois Alliance Library System received LSTA funding to develop a safety manual and accompanying workshops. Together the two groups of librarians crafted appropriate policies for the MyWebLibrarian service that were incorporated into the safety manual section on "Virtual or E-mail Problem Customer." Comparative research is needed on the type and frequency of abuse in the virtual environment versus the physical library.

There may also be different types of questions that librarians are asked in a VR service. In an evaluation of the cooperative academic library Ready for Reference Service, Sloan (2001) noted that the average length of a reference session was just over thirteen minutes. Most of the questions were ready-reference, though some were in-depth and provided an opportunity for instruction. Elias and Morrill (2003) observe that VR is not necessarily the best method for conducting in-depth research interviews with patrons, and in such instances, virtual reference may be seen as the doorway into the library's other public services; moreover, what a patron needs may be in the print collection of the library or archives.

The types of questions asked in various virtual reference services have run the gamut, though it is thought that questions an individual may be too embarrassed to ask in person become easier to put forth in the virtual environment. Librarians working VR may receive many more sexually explicit questions than they would get on the traditional reference desk.

## WORKING FROM HOME

Once a librarian has become acclimated to the virtual reference environment, often through a pilot project at the library, s/he may find this a thoroughly enjoyable means of passing hours outside of work. One of the advantages of working virtual reference is that it can be done from home. The person on the other end of a session does not know or care if the librarian is in Australia or central Illinois, dressed in a business suit or pajamas. The evening and weekend hours and working at home might appeal to a librarian with young children who wants to stay home, but still needs to work. Virtual reference provides job opportunities for librarians who are geographically bound with few traditional library work opportunities.

One librarian responded that "working at home is great; it breaks up my day and allows me to pick up my kids from school . . . No downside to it." Another librarian stated, "The flexibility of delivering reference services from home is wonderful." Another added, "It's quieter at home and I am less likely to be disturbed . . . generally a more pleasant atmosphere than my office." Some librarians liked being able to work evening and weekend hours without having to drive to the office. If a librarian is working from home and the service is not busy, the librarian can do other tasks while waiting for questions. Patrons also are often multitasking as well. As VR services become more popular, or if the librarian is monitoring numerous libraries, it can be a challenge to keep up with all the questions, and the librarian may have more than one session going at a time.

## CHALLENGES OF WORKING VIRTUAL REFERENCE AT HOME

Regardless of where the VR librarian is physically located, VR presents some challenges. Kenney (2003) summarizes the list of challenges articulated by the VR librarians at the Cleveland Public Library: "steep learning curve, with some psychological stress, databases that are cumbersome to use, older technology on the user's end, patrons with poor writing skills that hamper the process, and occasional rudeness."

One of the challenges of working virtual reference from home on a contract basis is that the librarian provides the computer and pays for an Internet connection and electricity. Work and home environments become mixed. Compared to traditional reference, the costs of providing a

VR service are borne more by the individual librarian. A librarian performing VR from home does not have access to the array of print resources available to a librarian working at a library. Communication with other colleagues is not personal and immediate, but can be done via e-mail, instant messaging, or phone. According to the librarians who responded to the survey, not having colleagues to consult with in person was a definite challenge and downside to working VR from home. Resources consulted are confined to the electronic. There may be more distractions at home than working at the office. Young children may not understand that a parent keyboarding on the computer is "at work." Even if a librarian works well independently, and consults with colleagues, working at home can be isolating. If the service is busy, the librarian is tied to the computer, making it hard to take a break. Another challenge may be a slower Internet connection.

Another potential downside to doing virtual reference work on a contract basis is that since the work is on a contract basis, there are not the usual benefits a librarian would expect even in a part-time job. Working on contract, librarians have to pay their own social security; taxes are not deducted from the paycheck.

## WHICH DO LIBRARIANS PREFER AND WHY?

In our survey, 55 of the 58 overall respondents answered the question about which type of reference work they enjoy more. Twenty-three librarians (42 percent) preferred traditional reference work; twenty-two (40 percent) enjoyed both; and ten (18 percent) enjoyed virtual reference more. For the librarians who liked both, they enjoyed the variety of providing reference services in different ways. One librarian stated, "In VR, I miss the visual clues." A typical comment from librarians who enjoyed both was that in providing service in different ways, the patron has more access to the library and can ask a reference question at a place (physical or Internet) which is most comfortable for them. A few librarians stated that VR was just another way of providing reference services and that it was important for reference librarians to be familiar with all types of service: the traditional desk, e-mail, phone, and virtual reference.

For those who prefer traditional reference, the face-to-face and personal contact is extremely important. In our survey, one librarian remarked, "I'm one who doesn't use bank machines or self-service checkouts because I like to interact with people I can speak with." The visual cues and body language in an in-person reference interview can assist the librarian greatly in helping a library patron; the librarian can more easily tell if they are finding the information a patron needs. In an in-person transaction, the librarian has access to a more complete array of print and electronic resources. One librarian preferred traditional reference because the librarian could provide more library instruction for the patron in showing them how to use resources.

## *WORKING IN A COOPERATIVE VIRTUAL REFERENCE ENVIRONMENT*

Many of the virtual reference services are cooperative which means that librarians covering the desk are answering questions for a number of libraries at any given time. Answering questions from another library may be frustrating because it becomes necessary to search their Web site for policies or local information. Elias and Morrill (2003) observe that remembering all of the policies and procedures of the member libraries of a reference consortium can be difficult. Some information needs are local. Various libraries may have different databases, so the VR librarian has to be familiar with what is offered by each.

As traditional library reference desks continue to attract people who are library users, the virtual reference setting may introduce an entirely new user group to the library and information resources. Students who are reluctant library users may be more likely to use the library online than to come to the reference desk. The ability to assist students or patrons during times when the library is not open or for someone who does not have easy or ready access to a library is extremely rewarding and, again, reaches out to potentially new library users. Kenney (2003) notes, "It's not about choosing between physical libraries or virtual ones. It's about making both available to suit different users, at different times." With virtual reference services, there are no geographic or physical barriers for the patron or the librarian.

Some librarians liked the text chat and co-browsing and used the opportunity to demonstrate online resources for the patron. A high percentage of questions in the virtual setting are from school-aged children; they are used to the Internet. A wider variety of patrons in age, economic background and interests come in person to the library. Several librarians stated that it was easier for a virtual patron to become impatient and demanding of the librarian. One librarian who labeled himself/herself as an introvert, preferred the virtual environment because it was less tiresome than providing traditional reference; however, this same librarian said if he/she were only doing VR, he/she would miss the human contact.

At this time, it is too soon to tell if working full time as a virtual reference librarian would be professionally satisfying. The librarians responding to our survey indicated that virtual reference was a part of their regular or full-time duties in the library. Two librarians indicated they performed virtual reference on a contract basis. Companies such as Tutor.com who employ librarians on a contract basis to do virtual reference primarily hire part-time staff people. One librarian who thought at one time that working VR from home would be the ideal career choice indicated that she changed her mind when she realized it would mean she would be tied to a computer eight hours a day.

## CONSULTATION WITH COLLEAGUES WHILE WORKING VR

Consultation with colleagues while doing VR greatly varies depending on whether the librarian is doing VR from home or from the library. While doing VR in the library, the librarian can easily consult with others on staff in-person. Consulting with colleagues while working from home can be done over the phone, but more often is done by using instant messaging with others on the same shift or by opening another chat window in the VR software. When working for a commercial reference service provider, colleagues working the same shift may be located anywhere in the United States or the world, so consultation has to be done on the computer. Questions that cannot be easily answered are forwarded via e-mail to a subject expert. In some libraries, there are regular meetings on VR where transcripts are shared and analyzed.

## MOST POPULAR RESOURCES USED

The most popular and useful resource in providing virtual reference services is Google, the Internet search engine. Other commonly consulted resources for virtual reference librarians include the online catalog and electronic databases subscribed to by the library. A number of librarians indicated that many of the answers to questions from VR sessions could be found in freely available sources on the Internet. Librarians providing services for academic libraries relied more on electronic databases than public library services.

## *WORKING FOR A COMMERCIAL REFERENCE PROVIDER*
### *versus A LIBRARY*

All but one of the respondents to the survey worked virtual reference as a part of their regular library job. One respondent did VR work in their regular job and on contract for a commercial reference provider. When working for a commercial reference provider that offers back-up reference services such as tutor.com or 24/7, most of the librarians work part-time on a contract basis. Hours worked are mainly evening and weekend hours. The advantages of working for a commercial provider include the opportunity for a librarian who works in another area of the library arena to keep abreast of new technologies and maintain reference skills.

## *JOB POSITION AVAILABLE:*
## *VIRTUAL REFERENCE SERVICE MANAGER*

As virtual reference services continue to spring up around (the world is not flat) the world, so do job advertisements that seek a librarian to manage the new service. The jobs may comprise the coordination of a VR service at a single institution or for a collaborative service. In order to share costs and desk coverage, libraries are increasingly partnering to provide VR; therefore, more managerial positions may become available for cooperative efforts.

There are two keys to success for a librarian in managing a virtual reference project. The first is to keep scrupulous track of the smallest details. The addition or deletion of a single librarian from a group providing VR service can result in changes to all the schedules, listservs, user accounts, and documents associated with the project. If new libraries are joining an existing consortium, they will need to be trained, get technical support contacts and various pieces of documentation, desk duty and committee assignments. Librarians need to write careful notes and reminders and keep good records of the progress or status of an event or process. Personnel at vendors, member institutions, and any number of other associated organizations change frequently. Updated contact lists are important as soon as a change occurs.

The second key is to be as organized as possible. Librarians need to analyze carefully what the major activity categories are, then create computer directories for each to store electronic files. Contents should be reviewed from time to time and drafts, outdated, or superceded material should be deleted. Librarians need to establish and follow procedures for all appropriate activities by using worksheets, timetables, or checklists. Anticipation and planning are critical. Confirmation of appointments and checking on arrangements a day or two ahead of time is a must for a librarian managing a VR project.

In addition to those major points, there are several minor skill sets that can contribute to the successful management of a VR project. A project manager frequently deals with directors or supervisors at higher levels and librarians actually staffing the service who may do VR duty on a voluntary basis. The ability to treat both groups with courtesy and tact make it easier to solve problems or ask for favors. Follow up as soon as possible on any promises to check into something or find out more information. A good manager/coordinator is knowledgeable about both the hardware and software technology being used and continuously updates that knowledge and strives to accumulate more. In the VR world things can happen quickly so the ability to react quickly and think flexibly can prevent a problem from developing into a crisis.

## QUALITY OF SERVICE
## OR WHAT IS A NICE LIBRARIAN
## DOING IN A PLACE LIKE THIS?

Librarians, whether in the electronic or traditional reference setting, try to provide their patrons with the best answer available in a courteous, professional manner. Can a librarian provide the same quality of service in an electronic environment as they can in an in person encounter? The answer is not a simple yes or no. Technology, though constantly improving and attaining higher levels of reliability, does not always work as smoothly as desired. The virtual reference librarian may have the latest equipment and the fastest Internet connection available, but the patron probably doesn't. Even with occasional downtimes, glitches, slow response time, and equipment failure, a majority of patrons using MyWebLibrarian, a virtual reference service provided by forty Illinois libraries, were very satisfied with their results. Several variables determine the success of any reference transaction. As much as it pains any of us to admit it, we all know there are times when our co-workers and even ourselves do not provide the best answer available with a smile on our faces. The reasons range from lack of experience or knowledge to lack of enthusiasm. The general knowledge, training and resourcefulness of the librarian are keys to the quality of any service. In the electronic format, the librarian's skills are in the spotlight.

The success of the online reference transaction depends on the librarian's abilities. The skill to correctly interpret the client's question is the first step. Next the practitioner must quickly determine a search strategy, locate an accurate answer using Internet resources and online databases; and share the results in a timely fashion. The professional must convey all of these components in a friendly, helpful manner without the assistance of body language or spoken cues. This may sound like a tall order requiring the skills of a super hero. Yet, many in the library profession do this and do it well everyday.

The virtual environment shifts the emphasis of the reference experience away from the physical structure of the library and focuses it on the librarian. Many library professionals wonder if they and their staff or colleagues are up to the challenge. Beyond completing basic training, how can an individual prepare to be a good virtual librarian?

The first thing to do is to not panic or feel intimidated. An average librarian already has most of the required talents. The skills and experience library staff employ every day at the traditional reference desk transfer well to virtual reference. Negotiating the reference question, knowing the best source to find the answer, and anticipating client needs serve a librarian well in any setting.

The second component is practice. With practice comes confidence. The librarian must commit to a schedule of practice. The best practice situation occurs with a mentor who is an experienced virtual reference practitioner. The mentor can provide the benefit of their experience with helpful tips, suggestions, and ideas for improvement. If this is not possible, then practice partners should be varied. Broader experience in training sessions better help prepare the knowledge professional for the realities of providing the actual service.

The third element is attitude. Whether one volunteers or is "drafted" into the ranks of virtual librarianship, the more willing the librarian is to give the experience a fair trial the better their chance of succeeding. Some of the participating librarians in MyWebLibrarian admit they were dubious about virtual reference, but they have come to enjoy providing the service and are excellent advocates. A few of the participants feel that their reference skills have been honed by the experience.

Once training and preparation are complete and the project is up and running, how can the quality of the service be evaluated? Whether the library is providing the service alone, with other library partners, or using a commercial service to help cover hours, the best way to determine the project's effectiveness is to ask the users. A patron satisfaction survey that pops up or is given as an option at the end of the reference transaction is very useful. To be helpful, the survey must ask the right questions while not being too long or complicated for the user to quickly complete. The favorable comments provide reassurance to the librarians and reaffirm their skills. The negative comments are informative in detailing what needs improvement.

The survey is only one measure. It might not catch the truly displeased who just give up on the experience and disconnect. According to MyWebLibrarian survey results, many virtual users are not traditional library patrons. They are unfamiliar with the services that librarians and libraries can provide them. Some virtual patrons are just grateful to get any help they can with wading through the plethora of information available on the Web. It is important for the project manager to monitor the transactions.

Many software products allow for more than one person to be on the virtual "desk" at one time. The manager should at least take an occasional shift. This allows them to experience the service, warts and all, first hand. The manager develops credibility with the information providers and a deeper understanding of the pressures and pleasures that accompany staffing the service.

Some software packages allow for an administrator to be a silent third party who can observe both the librarian and patron sides of the reference transaction. Another helpful software feature to utilize in quality assurance and continuous quality improvement (CQI) techniques is the ability of the librarian and the service manager to review a complete written transcript of each reference exchange. These tools are very useful in determining best practices as well as needed training. In traditional reference service, this level of CQI has not been possible and may initially be intimidating to a virtual reference librarian, who wonders if this will factor into her annual performance review. The authors feel that transcripts should be used to evaluate and improve the service and should not in any way be factored into individual performance reviews. Some services have team meetings, in which each VR librarian furnishes an example of a session s/he was particularly pleased with, and one that was somewhat lacking. The patron information is deleted for confidentiality, and the entire team of VR librarians reviews and offers suggestions to each other.

Careful consideration must be given to who is given administrator privileges. In MyWebLibrarian, the two project directors, the project coordinator, and each participating library are given the ability to appoint one administrator for each library. The intent of this action is to provide each library manager the ability to monitor his or her own staff. A few individuals who are not the coordinator started to monitor other libraries besides their own and offer suggestions for improvement. Needless to say, this created some disquiet among the partner libraries. This forced the group to discuss the issue, develop a deeper level of trust, and respect the coordinator's role as well as determine the responsibility of each library administrator. Gaining the commitment of each library to periodically monitor their staff is helpful to ensure quality service. It is best done locally because training issues can be dealt with more promptly. This is especially useful in a consortium or busy services. If the coordinator does not have this back-up team, he or she must develop a schedule to do sporadic monitoring of transactions.

In a particularly busy service, it is impossible for anyone to monitor every transaction. A random sampling of transcripts can prove very useful. One method is to once a month take 100 to 200 queries and carefully examine every fifth one in detail. This provides a fairly accurate sketch of trends and patterns in the service. Information achieved by this method should be verified by polling the participants of the service to determine its accuracy.

Another monitoring method is to recruit friends, family, and acquaintances to use the service and report their experiences. Amazingly enough this often provides a good cross section of the general public in regards to age, sex, and education. This is probably the least scientific way to gather data, but it can be quite illuminating especially if you ask the recruits to be painfully honest. It can also be useful for the coordinator to pose as a patron and ask each shift or participant to answer the same question. This proves there is more than one method or single resource to use to get an accurate answer. It is very useful to glean a list of resources and strategies used by the librarians to answer the question and to share it with the group. To do this most efficiently, the participants should create an electronic mailing list or an online group or community of practice to share information and discuss issues.

The key to creating a successful and vital virtual reference service is to seek active member involvement. As participants develop a sense of pride and ownership in the project, their commitment to providing the highest level of service and creating a value added product increases. The value of the service to its users also expands.

After participating in the creation, development, and expansion of a reference service, it is easy to predict that eventually virtual reference will be as prevalent as telephone reference is today. The technology will change but the concept will remain. It is vital that librarians go beyond the bricks and mortar of their library buildings and meet their patrons at their point of need. Virtual reference is currently the best way to reach this goal. Another benefit is that it provides librarians an opportunity to showcase their talents and be more of a presence in their communities.

Indeed, text-chat reference may represent a transitional phase as better means of reaching patrons at their point of need are developed. Voice capability is already present in several products. Video will follow. Text-chat may remain a key component for quite some time. As co-operative services become multi-lingual and multi-national, text may remain the easiest way to communicate across languages, especially if translation devices continue to be improved. Although there are several languages represented in the VR environment, it may be some time before a service can offer access to all languages. At the same time, as microphones and video become more common in homes and libraries and broadband becomes more capable and available, VR librarians may be communicating to users through voice and video, and still pushing them electronic information. Perhaps when the text or voice of one language can be translated to the voice of another, we will indeed have arrived at a new level of information provision!

## ADVICE FOR LIBRARIANS
## WHO WANT TO WORK VIRTUAL REFERENCE

Librarians working virtual reference offered some advice for librarians who want to try working VR or who are new to VR. "Enjoy the ride, we're at the beginning of something big and there's no telling where it will end up!" stated one respondent. Another thought that VR services were an exciting opportunity for librarians. A librarian urged others to use the co-browsing feature since it is "a wonderful opportunity to guide a patron through an information quest." Several librarians responded that the basic skills to be a good reference librarian in the traditional setting and the VR setting are the same, that what is important is conducting a good reference interview and getting the patron the information they need. Some librarians felt that VR is exciting, cutting edge, and

Hollywood; others advised not to do it just because it seems "sexy," and not to think of VR services as "exotic" because they are not. If a librarian thinks they might like VR, but is not sure, he or she could set up an instant messaging account and use that to see if VR might be enjoyable. Librarians urged new VR librarians to try it, to get as much training as possible, and to join a VR electronic list to share information with others and keep up with new developments. Many cautioned that to be a good VR librarian, you need to be a good traditional reference librarian. We will need to wait and see if a generation of "born VR" librarians provides good, solid reference service when considered in some absolute sense, regardless of environment and medium. Just because someone might be good at technological venues does not make them a good reference librarian.

Tennant (2003) notes that the interesting aspects of VR are not the features of the software or the pricing models of the vendors, but the practical and philosophical issues surrounding VR services. The idea of VR as a good career is at once both practical and philosophical. Could a librarian have a successful and rewarding career founded on providing VR services through a library, a consortium, a vendor, or as a rogue reference provider? It may be too soon to tell. As Tennant (2003) notes, "It is the curious, nettlesome, and sometimes aggravating mix of eminently practical and sublimely philosophical questions raised by VR that make it fascinating." So, in summary, it really is difficult at this point in the development of VR to determine if a predominantly VR service environment would be an effective service program that is professionally rewarding for the service providers.

## REFERENCES

Balleste, Roy, and Gordon Russell. 2003. Hollywood Technology in Real Life. *Computers in Libraries* 23, 4 (April): 14-16, 18.
*Safe Harbor: Policies and Procedures for a Safe Library*. Ed. by Rose M. Chenoweth. Pekin, IL: Alliance Library System, 2003.
Coffman, Steve. 2003. *Going Live: Starting & Running a Virtual Reference Service*. Chicago, IL: American Library Association. Includes a bibliography contributed by Bernie Sloan.
Coffman, Steve. 2002. What's Wrong with Collaborative Digital Reference? *American Libraries* 33, 11 (December): 56-58.
Elias, Tana, and Stef Morrill. 2003. Our Virtual Reference Training Camp: Testing the Players Before Signing Them On. *Computers in Libraries* 23, 4 (April): 10-12, 70-72.

Jacso, Peter. 2003. Virtual Reference Service and Disservice. *Computers in Libraries* 23, 4 (April): 52-54.

Kenney, Brian. 2003. The Virtual Gets Real. *Library Journal* (September 15): 32-35.

Lipow, Anne Grodzins. 2003. The Virtual Reference Librarian's Handbook. Neal-Schuman.

Meola, Mark, and Sam Stormont. 2002. Starting and Operating Live Virtual Reference Services.

Pace, Andrew. 2003. Virtual Reference: What's in a Name? *Computers in Libraries* 23, 4 (April): 55-56.

Sloan, Bernie. 2001. Ready for Reference: Academic Libraries Offer Live Web-Based Reference Evaluating System Use. Available online, http://www.lis.uiuc.edu/~b-sloan/r4r.final.htm.

Sloan, Bernie. 2003. My Web Librarian: A Report on Patterns of System Use and User Satisfaction. Available online http://www.myweblibrarian.com.

Tennant, Roy. 2003. Revisiting Digital Reference. *Library Journal*, 128, 1 (January 1): 38, 40.

White, Marilyn Domas, Eileen G. Abels, and Neal Kaske. 2003. Evaluation of Chat Reference Service Quality: Pilot Study. *D-Lib Magazine* 9, 2. Available online http://www.dlib.org/dlib/february03/white/02white.html.

White, M.D. (2001). Digital reference services: Framework for analysis and evaluation. *Library & Information Science Research*, 23, 211-231.

## APPENDIX. Virtual Reference Librarianship Survey

- Name and email address (or anonymous)

- How many hours per week do you work virtual reference?
  - 1-5
  - 6-10
  - 11-15
  - 15-20
  - 20 or more

- Do you work virtual reference on a contract basis, as part of your regular full-time job or both?

- If you work virtual reference from home, what do you like most about it? What do you like least?

- What do you think are the most important skills for a virtual reference librarian? Do you feel any of these are unique from traditional reference librarianship?

- Do you consult with colleagues while doing VR work? If so, what methods do you use to communicate?

- What type of reference work do you enjoy more? VR or traditional? Why?

- What online sources do you most commonly use while doing VR?

- Please add any thoughts on working VR or advice for others considering this type of work.

# Evolving Reference, Changing Culture: The Dr. Martin Luther King, Jr. Library and Reference Challenges Ahead

## Harry Meserve

**SUMMARY.** Analyzes the new Dr. Martin Luther King, Jr. Library in San Jose, California in terms of the experience in developing new ideas and confronting new problems in reference service. Argues that developing a merged public-university reference service encounters important problems that are similar to the challenges that face reference services everywhere in the 21st century. Introduces the problem of how a merged public-academic reference service must develop a new reference culture in order to succeed. Links the development of the reference culture to the ideas of Life Long Learning and Information Literacy. *[Article copies available for a fee from The Haworth Document Delivery Service: 1-800-HAWORTH. E-mail address: <docdelivery@haworthpress.com> Website: <http://www.HaworthPress.com> © 2006 by The Haworth Press, Inc. All rights reserved.]*

**KEYWORDS.** Merged public-academic libraries, merged reference service, new model library, reference culture, future of reference, economies of scale, budget constraints, library politics, Life Long Learning, Information Literacy

---

Harry Meserve is Reference and Instruction Librarian, Dr. Martin Luther King, Jr. Library, San Jose State University, One Washington Square, San Jose, CA 95192 (E-mail: hmeserve@sjsu.edu).

[Haworth co-indexing entry note]: "Evolving Reference, Changing Culture: The Dr. Martin Luther King, Jr. Library and Reference Challenges Ahead." Meserve, Harry. Co-published simultaneously in *The Reference Librarian* (The Haworth Information Press, an imprint of The Haworth Press, Inc.) No. 93, 2006, pp. 23-42; and: *New Directions in Reference* (ed: Byron Anderson, and Paul T. Webb) The Haworth Information Press, an imprint of The Haworth Press, Inc., 2006, pp. 23-42. Single or multiple copies of this article are available for a fee from The Haworth Document Delivery Service [1-800-HAWORTH, 9:00 a.m. - 5:00 p.m. (EST). E-mail address: docdelivery@haworthpress.com].

## INTRODUCTION

### The Dr. Martin Luther King, Jr. Library and New Conceptions of Reference Service

An understanding of the new realities of reference work–the present and future of reference–begins with a look at the ways in which "reference" is defined. Reference librarians need to know and understand the factors that condition their ability to do reference and how these factors will change in the years ahead. One way to take the measure of reference today is to look at the development of a "new model library," conceived by its designers as "a library like no other, for a community like no other."[1] Such a library is the new Dr. Martin Luther King, Jr. Library, recently opened on the corner of 4th Street and San Fernando Street in the city of San Jose, California.

Opened on August 1, 2003, the new King library is an example of a project that was conceived out of fiscal necessity. Its planning survived some fairly intense politicking, and now comes to fruition in a time of budgetary crisis. It is part of a larger downtown scheme ("revitalization") being pursued by the city of San Jose. It developed, beginning in 1996, out of a need for a new main library for the city of San Jose and for a new academic library at San Jose State University, the city's campus of the California State University system. The joint-use library had its origins in fiscal necessity. It was believed that such a library would provide "economies of scale" and would be cheaper than building two libraries.

Because the library only opened recently, firm and long-standing conclusions about the possibilities of reference service in the new building cannot be drawn. What can be looked at is the way that the building itself shaped and impacted reference service. Also, how the decisions made attempted to create a library in which reference services (as well as the library as a whole) would begin to serve new populations in a new way, today and in the future.

The most important aspect of the new library was not its size (the largest library built all at one time west of the Mississippi River) or attractiveness, but its attempt to merge the functions of the main branch of a large urban public library (the Dr. Martin Luther King, Jr., "Main" Branch of the San Jose Public Library) with the Robert D. Clark Library at San Jose State University (SJSU). The merger of these two libraries was in itself a challenge to basic ideas that the library community has held about library service over the years, especially over the compatibility of the missions of academic and public libraries. The merger also provides an opportunity to see in practice how reference librarians can go about putting into effect conceptions that have been long held about how reference service will change over the years.

## THE NEW DR. MARTIN LUTHER KING, JR. LIBRARY AND THE ROAD AHEAD FOR REFERENCE

### Town and Gown: The University and the Community

The new Dr. Martin Luther King, Jr. Library began as an idea about how to deal with two libraries, both of which were in need of modernization and enlargement. It was, of course, noted from the start that the two existing libraries had different missions. The Robert D. Clark Library existed to support the curriculum of the university and to promote the research work of its faculty and students. School libraries (at all levels) support the curriculum of their schools and are thus centered on the tasks of teaching and learning, in the university's case, the tasks of higher education and research. In a school library, especially a university library, librarians are guided by the main tasks of their daily work: giving direction, guidance and instruction to the research needs of faculty and students.

The (old) Dr. Martin Luther King, Jr. Library was the downtown branch and the headquarters of a large and expanding city library system. The city of San Jose comprises an extremely diverse community of over 925,000 people (largest city in the San Francisco Bay Area and second largest city in the state of California). The San Jose Public Library has eighteen branches and a bookmobile and is growing, due to a special tax-for-libraries passed by the people of the city in recent years.

A public city library has a different mission from most school and university libraries. It seeks to meet the needs of the whole community for information, but also for public meeting rooms, computers accessible to all, "a clean well-lighted" place to read, literacy programs, children's services, etc. For public librarians, the daily routine is quite different from that of university librarians. The work of the public librarian is centered on the needs of the whole community, or at least that part of the community that uses the library and its outreach programs. Librarians provide a wider range of services and tend (in the reference area) to deliver requested information to patrons, rather than teaching how to find information for themselves.

This contrast between academic and public reference work flows not from theory, but from the needs of patrons and their habits of mind. A public librarian helps a patron ("customer" finds itself in use today in some libraries) find the latest in books on the California Missions because (s)he needs to help her child complete a school assignment. The librarian proposes self-help legal books to someone wishing to begin divorce proceedings. These are only two examples. For academic librarians, the substance and essence of reference work is not the conducting of research itself (not even the determination of certain basic facts), but helping patrons to conduct research for themselves. From the lecturer who needs access to chemistry databases to the student who has to find a "scholarly" article from a peer-reviewed journal, these are typical of reference users.

In public library work, the most stern reprimands are reserved for those librarians and staff who fail to deliver promised services in a timely way and with a good spirit. That is, patrons expect, and librarians are trained to deliver, information and services. These services include not only reference and information of all kinds, but also other kinds of services to people who have particular needs (children's programming, popular materials for seniors, literacy efforts, etc.). In a special sense, the difference between the university library and the public library is the difference between what has traditionally been termed "town" and "gown." That is, the university has traditionally been a part of the community in which it exists while at the same time being separate and apart from that community. It has a special function: learning, job preparation, research, and as a place where intellectual life is valued, preserved and sheltered. Students, staff, and faculty regularly cross the line between "town and gown," but all are aware that the atmosphere and "culture" of the university differs in quality from the civil community in which it resides.

The above could be the subject of a long essay in itself, but it is sufficient to point out that what is expected at the university library by its patrons, and what is expected at the public library by its patrons are two different things. Not only this, but the exchange of information takes place within differing cultural contexts. The university emphasizes instruction and the necessity of building a culture of learning. The librarian's work takes place in a predominantly collegial atmosphere, where students, staff and faculty all share the same goals within the context of the university. The public library emphasizes service, responding immediately to patron requests, and the need to speak to community needs. The public librarian operates within a context where the whole breadth and variety of the wider community, including its stresses and strains, is expressed directly at the Reference Desk and throughout the library.

### Town and Gown: The New Dr. Martin Luther King, Jr. Library

In the case of the new King Library, a number of theories were put forward to explain how the traditional and pervasive differences between academic and public libraries could be resolved in the new facility. Some early opposition by a small but vociferous part of the San Jose State faculty (centered around the Department of History), and ongoing discussions with librarians, staff, and others in the community and the university sharpened the dialogue and forced everyone involved in the project to deal with planning issues as they came up. The response was to develop a concept of the new library that would satisfy both university critics and explain the library to the public as well.

## TECHNOLOGICAL, BUDGETARY AND DEMOGRAPHIC CHANGES AND THE ORGANIZATION AND DEFINITION OF REFERENCE SERVICES

### Changing Libraries

Libraries have increasingly come under pressure to change resulting from a long list of technological, budgetary and demographic impacts that have severely tested the ability to provide service, given the structure of libraries themselves. Librarians struggle to cope with changes in the world outside their doors and (sometimes) lament the changes themselves. There are a whole range of problems faced by libraries: homelessness, filtering, government snooping, budget problems, pressure to justify library financing using models more appropriate to business, the cost of academic periodicals, management of Internet computers, and how to integrate new technologies into the established physical plant and organization of the library. The newspapers seem to report almost daily some new situation that threatens to test once again librarians' ability to manage libraries.

These changes have changed the nature of library service (as seen from the point of view of our communities), and are reflections of bigger changes in the world. The homeless are not in libraries because they wish to be trouble. Their occasional disruption of library routine is not just a nuisance; it is also a reflection of the fact that the world creates more homeless people (due to economic changes and the closing of community places that used to help street people). This is true for many changes in library routine, made necessary by broad changes in social attitudes and values.

More to the point of this essay, the popularity of the Internet is both a reflection of the willingness of commercial, governmental, and educational institutions to promote its use, perhaps for their own corporate reasons. This causes a new kind of "information seeking" on the part of anyone who wants information today, regardless of whether the context is an academic or public library.

### Changing Reference

There is a great deal of discussion in the library world about changes librarians face, and of course, a whole literature has developed over the years about "what is to be done?" The interest here is to try to look at reference specifically and show how one library is moving towards new ideas about what librarians need to do in reference services. The definition of "reference" is in the process of changing, precisely because the nature of information and our ability to use it has been profoundly altered by technology that stores information and delivers it to the user.

Librarians have the ability to access a larger and larger universe of information. The technology necessary to acquire the information is more available, not only in libraries and other storehouses of information, but in all manner of businesses and private spaces. Processing the information is in the hands of corporate, governmental and educational providers. In the present system, the availability of information is conditioned mainly by the ability of the user to find the appropriate resource and desired information, and to evaluate the information acquired. Reference librarians are used to answering "ready reference" kinds of questions and these seem still the central reason for the existence of the librarian and the reference desk. More and more, however, in all kinds of libraries, the experience is that patrons have a greater need for searching and evaluating skills (the skills which are the strength of librarians) than they have for specific bits of information.

There is strong evidence of this in the falling reference desk statistics that are reported by some libraries and in the perceived experience of reference librarians themselves. Librarians find that patrons think of the information provided by the commercial Internet (especially the Web) with a perhaps unwarranted faith in its accuracy and currency. Because they can easily access Internet information, the information itself appears to be more reliable, or at least usable, than it really is.

The recent and widely-read study by the Pew Internet & American Life Project, entitled, "Use of the Internet at Major Life Moments," demonstrates this tendency to rely on the Internet. The study showed that Americans, who were experiencing major life decisions, were turning to the Internet to help provide themselves with information in times of the most personal and private need.[2] The whole culture of the Internet– the fact that one does not have to ask another person for information but can get the information by their own efforts with results specific to themselves, etc.–creates a situation in which "traditional" reference question-answering functions will likely decline, but the real skills of librarianship will likely become more valuable.

Reference librarians cease to be the only experts on where to find the answer to specific reference questions in the immediate sense. In the same moment, they become the experts on how to find information resources, how to access them, and how to evaluate the results of our searches. This is what libraries and librarians have always done best. Technology has given us a new arena in which to contribute our skills.

In the near term, reference will be dominated by the Internet and all of its functions (e-mail, OPACs, online databases, community Web resources, search engines, etc.). The technological environment librarians function in is sure to be one of rapid development and diversity. The consequent function of that part of the library still called "reference" is even more clearly needed to provide the expertise and guidance that patrons of all kinds, from all communities, will need to navigate the growing flood of information.

## *CREATING A SEAMLESS, "UNDIFFERENTIATED" REFERENCE SERVICE*

The decision to build a new building and merge the San Jose Main Library and the SJSU library within its walls was made over a period of two years between 1996 and 1998. The political decision to move ahead followed the completion of feasibility studies in 1997, then the writing of the formal Memorandum of Understanding in 1998. Fundamentally, the decision was based on fiscal necessity (the promise of "economies of scale") and the objective need for new library buildings that could provide for growth over a twenty-five year span. Neither the City of San Jose nor San Jose State University could have afforded a new building, with all its promises of architectural beauty and a much more modern technological framework.

The process of decision-making required negotiation and careful consultation with staff, faculty, and the public. The largest question (so far as the university faculty were concerned) was whether or not public patrons would have access to academic collections. The decision was to give equal access to all patrons (albeit with different borrowing privileges), and that if this proved to be a problem in the future, new conditions could be negotiated.

The formation of merged units within the library's structure (reference was one of these) was consistent with the need to find economies of scale in the new organization. The rule of thumb was that services should be integrated except in cases where this was shown to be either uneconomical or not of value to the people who use the library. Thus, the idea of "seamless service" became the accepted rule of thumb. That is, patrons should not be able to tell the difference between (previously) public or university services. The services thus provided would not be qualitatively either "public" or "academic."

The decision to apply a seamless principle to the merging of reference services meant the creation of a reference service that would be staffed by librarians and support staff from both institutions. Its "seamlessness" in answering questions, providing search instruction on the desk (as well as direct answers to queries), and even moving toward a joint collection development policy for the reference collection, were all goals of the new library. The writing of a reference policy for the "Merged Reference Unit" (MRU, as it was called) took up the task of creating what one writer called, "One reference service for everyone."[3]

### Issues in Reference–Present and Future

When the planners of the reference unit in the new library began the process of conceiving and implementing a plan, they faced a wide range of difficulties. A section of the university faculty opposed the whole notion of combining public and academic services. They were concerned about the quality of reference services that would be available to them and their students. They considered requesting that university patrons be served only by university librarians. In addition, they wanted to be sure that their accustomed library borrowing privileges would be maintained. In general, there was genuine concern about the merging, not of the libraries per se, but in what they conceived of as the resulting change in quality and composition of services.

The planning process encompassed staff retreats, focus groups, and consultation at every step of the process. What seemed to lie at the center was the necessity of creating what was termed a "new culture" for reference. It was at times an emotionally charged question. Neither public librarians (with their ethic of service) nor academic librarians (with their ethic of instruction and collegiality) were eager to embrace a new (as yet undefined) reference style.

As the new Dr. Martin Luther King, Jr. Library begins to provide reference services, it will have to establish and articulate its own particular style of reference work. The model of reference that becomes the norm will have to be both consciously and practically a model that takes on the most important questions facing libraries in the 21st century.

## Reference Style, Reference Culture: Defining a New Norm

In preparation for work in the new library (before the new building was finished), discussions began on how the new reference unit would define itself. Should the new reference service be integrated or simply mirror a "separate but equal" replication of the two reference services, i.e., "Shall we have two reference desks or one?" How should librarians create guidelines for university and public librarians to work together?

The attempt to define a new reference culture began with studies conducted by Prof. Thomas Childers of Drexel University. His charge was to try to determine if the perceived gulf of difference between public and academic librarians was real. Based on a shadowing project, follow-up discussions and a questionnaire, Childers concluded that there was not as great a difference as had been assumed. So far as activity at the reference desk itself was concerned, he concluded, there were a number of conditions that would indicate a positive result in the proposed integration of public and academic reference librarians.

Both groups of librarians observed that the questions answered at the two reference desks were essentially similar and not requiring a depth of subject information. There was an overlap of patron groups (undergraduate students use the public as well as the academic library to complete their assignments) and questions from the public were often quite challenging.

## Question Answering

In Professor Childers' studies, it was determined that it was possible to contemplate and plan for a merged (academic and public) reference desk because the questions asked at public and academic reference desks were quite similar. He judged questions that were asked by two criteria: what he called "interchangeability" (could the question be asked in any kind of library?) and "depth of need" (are the questions asked ready reference or research type questions?). This was his conclusion:

> The vast bulk of questions I judged interchangeable. To a large extent, this is because the public library fields many questions that arise from students . . . (and, on "depth of need"): . . . I thought that analyzing the Depth of Need would provide some differentiation among the questions, and that the differentiation would correlate at an impressionistic level with the two different libraries. However, that was not the case. For the most part, it was difficult to discern the depth of the researcher's need. . . . It seems that the vast majority of questions required little depth.[4]

Yet taking the questions at face value, without judging the context in which the questions are asked, leads to a false conclusion about the problems of creating a viable reference service with two distinct groups of patrons.

Academic librarians emphasize the use of journals because they are more scholarly and subject-specific. More and more, access to academic journals can most economically be provided electronically, instead of in the traditional print format. Students have a need for critical thinking and assessment skills. Academic librarians must therefore teach conceptually at the reference desk, as well as in class and one-on-one. They have to be able to show the patron not only how to answer questions but also how to evaluate resources and perform the routine searching strategies which will provide them with adequate resources for their projects and assignments.

Public librarians offer more direct, fact-based answers, unencumbered by the need to teach the methodology of searching as a primary motivation. They are required to offer more breadth of service. Their time is more taken up with the sheer number of patrons and the need to answer a wide range of questions (directional, computers, quick reference, etc.). In order to answer as many questions as possible, there is a need to do triage at the reference desk.

It would be a mistake to make too much of the somewhat limited studies that were carried out on the comparative functions of librarians and on the nature of questions asked at a reference desk(s). What was legitimately shown was that the information needs of patrons at the reference desk were much more similar than the librarians would have predicted. A single, merged reference unit centered around work performed at a single reference desk (and a call center) was deemed possible. Two conditions were necessary to make such a conception work: first, that extensive training take place so that the operational skills of the two sets of librarians would become roughly uniform and at a high level. Second, that–in the process of working and training together–a new culture could evolve which could bridge the gap (both as perceived by both sets of librarians and as it actually existed) between the focus of library service in the two institutions.

The second goal, culture change, requires some thought and careful development. This is because a new "culture" has to amalgamate the values of the public library (service, equality of treatment) with those of the academic library (instruction, the development of scholarship). The library world has already faced the prospect of reinterpreting its understanding of reference in the face of computerization, digitization, multicultural issues, and profound changes in the ways in which patrons seek and make use of information.

The new Dr. Martin Luther King, Jr. Library has, by the mere fact of its creation at this time and in this place, become a test case. Is it possible to understand the profound changes taking place in the world around (and thus in the library world) and to develop a new orientation for reference work in the future?

## *ORGANIZATION AND CULTURE*

The slender bridge from two separate and different kinds of reference services to one merged reference unit was supplied by Professor Childers' report. From here, the Joint Library Reference Planning Team sponsored a series of organized planning retreats and a trip to a nearby university to see examples of different types of reference desks and facilities. The retreats informed a set of thirteen "Key Recommendations for the Design and Delivery of Reference Services at the Joint Library,"[5] which were put forward in October of 1999.

The recommendations provided for:

- a combined reference collection cataloged in Library of Congress mode;
- government publications to be inter-filed with the general reference collection and re-cataloged in Library of Congress call numbers, where possible;
- each institution to continue its own collection management decisions as before; and
- the separation of the merged reference collection into three distinct and separate areas ("pods") on the floor: Science, Social Sciences, and Humanities and Performing Arts, each focusing on reference services by subject.

Other recommendations were also made: the design of the escalator (reference to be on the second floor of the library), the shape of the reference desk, its location on the floor, facilities to accommodate patrons with disabilities, etc. The plan speaks of a "tiered references design" incorporating a First Floor Information Desk, the Reference Floor, and referrals of individuals to subject specialist librarians for further consultation.

This plan guided the development of the physical and architectural aspects of reference in the new Dr. Martin Luther King, Jr. Library (as it came to be referred to), though some aspects were not implemented (e.g., the "pod" concept). The other aspect of planning–the problem of merging two different "cultures" and creating one unified "Merged Reference Unit"–took longer.

### The Problem of Culture and Change

The problem of work-place culture is one about which much has been written and remarked upon in both the academic literature and in the study of practical aspects of the organization and management of enterprises, commercial, governmental, etc. The purpose of developing a "culture vision" for the new King Library was to find common ground between the experience and traditional functioning of the university library and the experience and normal functioning of the public library, a task that many would have considered a fool's errand. More specifically, the "culture vision" was defined as the basis on which the librarians and library staff of the two libraries could work together in the new building.

The problem facing the consultant hired to develop a method for merging the existing cultures of the two libraries was simple to understand: the actual work experience and values of the two institutions were, in fact, quite different. It became necessary, therefore, to invent a common ground and attempt to build consensus using this as a base. The method assessed the culture of each library, wrote a report, discussed the report with the library leadership, then published the report for discussion among the staff of both libraries. The report was an assessment of cultural similarities and differences between the two libraries, and a subsequent determination of which differences are severe enough to contribute toward becoming "barriers (to) achieving success in the new King Library."[6]

The report was intended to be discussed and refined, leading eventually to an implementation plan. In its initial phase, the report produced for discussion and further guidance: (1) a list of cultural attributes that are shared (between the two libraries); (2) a defined "Culture Vision Statement"; and (3) resultant "Core Purpose" and "Core Values." These are the basis for "Building a Shared/Blended Culture" for the new King Library.[7]

The whole cultural values development process took place over a period of almost fifteen months (August 2001 to November 2002). It involved a great deal of discussion, revision and refinement of the statements. In addition, it eventuated in the "Analysis of Organization and Staff Structures," "Proposed Options for Organization of Merged Functions," and a "Proposed Design and Implementation Plan" to carryout the process in the new King Library.[8]

There were considerable consultation, discussion and opportunities for input on these issues, especially on the practical issues of organization and shared management. As was said quite often, it was necessary for there to be considerable staff "buy in" for the project to be a success. But the difference in cultures will continue in the new library for an extended period of time. It is not possible outside the actual experience of working together to identify what real, lasting cultural values are coming from each institution, and which will survive in amended form in the new merged institution.

In the long run, it is sometimes true that it is the discussion of values and the discussion of change among employees and between management and employee, that are the most important factors in smoothing the way for change to take place. This is not to say that input is not substantial and valuable in making plans, but only that employees like to be consulted when it comes to substantial changes taking place in their working lives. There is a world of difference, however, between consultation on organizational issues and actual collaboration and mutual decision making between management and employees.[9]

## CREATING A NEW CULTURE:
## LIFE LONG LEARNING AND INFORMATION LITERACY

Now that the new Dr. Martin Luther King, Jr. Library has opened, it faces the test of fulfilling its promise in the 21st century. This promise is embodied in the demographics of two communities (the university and the city) and in the commitment to solve the problems that are inherent in the merging of reference services. The communities are extremely diverse–the public library alone collects books in over fifty languages. The library serves a population that wants both service and instruction. It provides a base for distance learning, for computer-based instruction, for insuring that computer skills and searching techniques become the property not only of the "literate 20 percent," but also of a much larger share of the population. There is an implicit goal of trying to contribute to the process of overcoming the "digital divide," a social problem of importance in this century.

The concept of Life Long Learning is given a new understanding in a library where the public patron may indeed be a professional engineer who has need of IEEE documents (which he could not have accessed in the old San Jose Main library). Or she may be an independent scholar researching Roman history, or a recently-graduated student who has learned the techniques of effective searching and wants to go on using them. Life Long Learning is not just for job changers and for seniors who return to reading and research. It is an idea of the library as an agent for the facilitation of the transition (in the individual and in the community) from formal to informal education.

Information Literacy–the other major goal of the new library–is embodied in the kind of "instruction" available in the library and through the library. It becomes a meeting place where students of all kinds see others (peers and elders) use the library, a place where learning can be pursued throughout life.

Life Long Learning and Information Literacy are concepts that are meant to define and promote the library's mission. Because of the demographics of our community and the technology that is now accessible, our patrons will now expect of us a library that will overcome the old divisions (between the academic and the public library, for example) and create a new paradigm. Concretely, because large sums have been spent on the construction of a new building, librarians will be expected to find ways to overcome the challenges of a combined reference service.

## What the Library Did

The new Dr. Martin Luther King, Jr. Library is in the forefront of a testing ground for merged reference services. In its self-conception, as illustrated in the planning documents, the King Library seeks to foster the development of a new and common culture. First, the library is physically laid out so as to combine "town and gown." Persons can enter onto the ground floor of the library coming either from the city (4th and San Fernando Streets in San Jose) or from the main part of the university campus. The ground floor itself is a "bridge" (a passageway) between city and campus. Merged services are accessible to all patrons, regardless of origin. Items from the two collections can be browsed by any patron, and materials are available to any patron for check out.

Second, an effort was made to study the "cultural" differences between public and university librarians and staff. Discussions, shadowing, problem-solving exercises, and joint project management efforts were all enlisted to create the basis for a new and common culture in the library. Finally, training and orientation efforts were carried out to try to prepare librarians and staff for the new work situation that they would face. Training was aimed at providing a common skill base to aid in the development of a "seamless" reference service.

## CONCLUSION

### Once Again, Town and Gown

Earlier in this paper, the differences in mission between the university and the public library were laid out. Ways were suggested in which the merged reference function in the new Dr. Martin Luther King, Jr. Library faced the challenge of resolving these differences, both in theory and practice, in the everyday world of reference work. The differences between "academic" and "public" reference work are analogous to the differences between the ways in which librarians do reference work (in general) today and how they will be called upon to do reference work in the future. There are the same distinctions between providing information and the teaching of search strategies, coupled with the evaluation of the relative value of various resources–both electronic and print. What is demanded of librarians by the increased domination of technology (in the library and everyday life) is a strong sense of how that technology impacts on human lives. Librarians cannot allow the technology to be the sole (or even the primary) determinant of how libraries react to the development of reference in the future.

### The Future of Reference Service

At the 2002 American Library Association's Annual Conference in Atlanta, the Reference and User Services Association (RUSA) sponsored a program entitled, "The Future of Reference Services." Five leaders in the organization of reference work presented papers and each of them directly or indirectly took up the question that has been raised in this paper.[10] What is striking is that these presentations, which reflected different points of view and different perspectives, all agreed on at least one theme: that the planning of reference services must keep in the forefront the needs of users and the necessity of adapting technological solutions to user needs. One could add that they would probably all agree that this kind of planning also necessitates the training (or re-training) of librarians in a culture of teaching and service.

Such a culture, the creation of which has been addressed in the planning documents for the new Dr. Martin Luther King, Jr. Library, is one that involves the conscious merging of the practice of public libraries with the priorities of academic libraries. This creates the possibility of "seamless" service, an ideal that is not yet expressed in reality.

David Tyckoson's contribution to the RUSA discussion was particularly pointed in its assertion that the basic functions of the reference librarian have not really changed even from the 19th century, i.e., "instruction, assisting with research, recommending sources, and promoting the library in the community. . . . " What is crucial, Tyckoson argues, is to understand that these functions will take place in a context of more sophisticated tools, an increased demand for instruction, and an increase in the diversity of the whole community, necessitating greater sophistication in the outreach function of the librarian. What is more, librarians will become more active in the creation (in different formats) and distribution of information sources for public and scholarly use.

The new Dr. Martin Luther King, Jr. Library is an experiment in the sense of being one of the most visible attempts to merge the functions and "cultures" of an academic library and those of a large urban main public library. The building is built and the library is open for business. What is not known, and will be more obvious in the next few years, is the degree to which the library will serve its new and diverse population in a "new way." This will include applying the ideas of Information Literacy and Life Long Learning, determining what model of reference service will become the norm in the new building, and whether a new "culture" of reference service can really be established. These questions confront reference librarians everywhere, challenging them to create a new idea of 21st century librarianship. What happens in the new King Library will be an indicator of the opportunities and problems that lie ahead.

## NOTES

1. Klingberg, Susan and Hutchinson, Sylvia. "A library like no other, for a community like no other" (brochure).
2. This is a story for another forum. I will not go into detail here, except to say that the SJSU/SJPL planners took all comments on the idea of the new King Library project seriously and engaged in community dialogue and decision-making to resolve differences, where possible.
3. See http://www.pewinternet.org/reports/toc.asp?Report=58.
4. Conaway, Peggy. "One Reference Service for Everyone?" *Library Journal* 125, 12 (July 2000): 42-44.
5. Childers, Thomas A. "Impressions of SJSU and SJPL queries at the desk" (photocopy of report) (July 6, 1999).
6. Pontau, Donna (for the Joint Library Reference Planning Team). (photocopy of report) (October, 1999).
7. For this and the previous paragraph, see Creth, Sheila. "A proposed culture vision for the new Dr. Martin Luther King, Jr. Library" (photocopy of report) (October, 2001).
8. "Organization and implementation plan for merged functions in the new King Library" (photocopy of report) (November 20, 2002).
9. There is a whole literature, going back at least to the "Hawthorne Studies" on workers at Western Electric in the 1920s, which speaks to the importance of consultation with employees and relationships between management and employees for positive morale and productivity. See, for example, Henderson, L.J., T.N. Whitehead and Elton Mayo. "The Effects of Social Environment," *International Journal of Public Administration* 21, no. 4 (1998): 589-404.
10. The five presentations from RUSA's "The Future of Reference Services Papers" have been reprinted in *Reference Services Review* 31, 1 (February 26, 2003).

## REFERENCES

Block, Marylaine. "Reference as a Teachable Moment." Ex Libris: an E-Zine, 146 (July 5, 2002). Available online, http://marylaine.com/exlibris/xlib146.html.
Chowdhury, G.G. "Digital Libraries and Reference Services: Present and Future." *Journal of Documentation* 58, 3 (2002): 258-83.

Conaway, Peggy. "One Reference Service for Everyone?" *Library Journal* 125, 12 (July 2000): 42-44.

Conaway, Peggy. "Shared Libraries." In *Encyclopedia of Library and Information Science* (May 20, 2003): 2636-2642.

Degele, Nina. "Knowledge in the Information Society." *World Futures* 49, 3 (September 1997): 743.

Janes. Joseph. "What is Reference For?" *Reference Services Review* 31, 1 (February 26, 2003): 22-25.

Kauppila, Paul and Russell, Sharon. "Economies of Scale in the Library World: The Dr. Martin Luther King Jr. Library in San Jose, California." *New Library World* 104, 7 (2003): 255-266.

Kommers, Nathan. Research Briefing: Use of the Internet at Major Life Moments. Pew Internet and American Life Project, May 8, 2002. Available online, http://www.pewinternet.org/reports/pdfs/PIP_Major_Moments_Report.pdf.

Lipow, Anne G. "Point-of-need Reference Service: No Longer an Afterthought." *Reference Services Review* 31, 1 (February 26, 2003): 31-36.

Radcliff, Carolyn J. "Issues for Information Desks in Academic Libraries: A Case Study." *Journal of Interlibrary Load, Document Delivery and Information Supply* 9, 1 (1998): 57-66.

Rettig, James. "Technology, Cluelessness, Anthropology and the Memex: The Future of Academic Reference Service." *Reference Services Review* 31, 1 (February 26, 2003): 17-21.

Tyckoson, David. "What is the Best Model for Reference Service?" *Library Trends* 50:2 (Fall 2001): 183.

Tyckoson, David. "On the Desireableness of Personal Relations Between Librarians and Readers: The Past and Future of Reference Service." *Reference Services Review* 31, 1 (February 26, 2003): 12-16.

Van Fleet, Connie. "The Free Lunch and the Future of Libraries." *RQ* 34, 2 (Winter 1994): 138.

Whitlatch, Jo Bell. "Reference Futures: Outsourcing, the Web, or Knowledge Counseling." *Reference Services Review* 31, 1 (February 26, 2003): 26-30.

APPENDIX. SJSU-SJPL Joint Library Documents

**June 17, 1999**

1. Marilyn Snider (facilitator). "SJPL/SJSU Reference and Instructional Services Strategic Planning Retreat" (on Mission Statement, Vision Statement, Core Values, Three Year Goals, Six Month Strategic Objectives, Next Steps).
2. Jo Bell Whitlatch. "Tiered Reference Services in the Joint Library" (prepared for retreat).

**July 6, 1999**

3. Thomas Childers. "Shadowing experience at the San Jose Public and San Jose University Libraries."
4. Thomas Childers. "Impressions of SJSU and SJPL queries at the desk."
5. Thomas Childers. "Perceptions of reference and instruction service tasks, academic vs. public."
6. Thomas Childers. "A questionnaire for selected staff of the SJSU and SJPL libraries."

**October, 1999**

7. Donna Pontau (for the Joint Library Reference Planning Team). "Recommendations for reference services and delivery."

**August, 2001**

8. Sheila Creth. "Organization culture assessment; SJSU Clark Library and SJPL."

**September 24, 2001**

9. Patricia Senn Breivik. "Culture Consultant's Report Follow-up."
10. "Clark Library Culture Statement" (with discussion).
11. Sheila Creth. "A proposed culture vision for the new Dr. Martin Luther King, Jr. Library."

**December, 2001**

12. "The Culture of the new Dr. Martin Luther King, Jr. Library" (Culture Vision Statement; Core Values, Revised).

**February, 2002**

13. "Draft Culture Statement of SJSU Library" (with Executive Summary).

**March, 2002**

14. Sheila Creth. "Human Resources Project: Analysis of organization and staff structures, San Jose Public Library & the San Jose State University Library" (Deliverable #1).

**April, 2002**

15. Sheila Creth. "Human Resources Project: Proposed options for organization of merged functions in the new Dr. Martin Luther King, Jr. Library" (Deliverable #2).

**June, 2002**

16. Sheila Creth. "Human Resources Project: Proposed design and implementation plan for organization of merged functions in the new King Library" (Deliverable #3).

**November, 2002**

17. "SJSU Library Strategic Plan 2002/2003" (November 16, 2002).
18. "Organization and implementation plan for merged functions in the new King Library" (November 20, 2002).

# Current Issues
# in Music Reference

## Michael Duffy IV

**SUMMARY.** The climate of change in music reference represents a challenge to librarians. The three issues in the library literature that probably have the greatest impact on music reference service and are the subject of this paper are changes in users, sources, and modes of access to sources. These three issues are certainly related, as users need to use sources, and they need to know how to access them in order to use them. Reference librarians are called upon to mediate this process. Music library collections have their own peculiarities, however. Because they contain a wider variety of materials than many other kinds of library collections, reference librarians for music collections must be aware of the format, content, and intended uses of these materials, as well as the research patterns of their patrons. In the recent past, as cultural norms have changed with the paradigm of Western culture, users have wanted to use music libraries in new ways, and librarians are challenged to accommodate them. The musical genres used and requested by today's library patrons are different than they once were, both for listening and for academic study. Musical reference sources are being issued in electronic formats, and this represents a challenge for some users. The expanded use of interlibrary loan and electronic access to materials

---

Michael Duffy IV is Music Librarian, Music Library, Northern Illinois University, DeKalb, IL 60115 (E-mail: mduffy@niu.edu).

[Haworth co-indexing entry note]: "Current Issues in Music Reference." Duffy IV, Michael. Co-published simultaneously in *The Reference Librarian* (The Haworth Information Press, an imprint of The Haworth Press, Inc.) No. 93, 2006, pp. 43-57; and: *New Directions in Reference* (ed: Byron Anderson, and Paul T. Webb) The Haworth Information Press, an imprint of The Haworth Press, Inc., 2006, pp. 43-57. Single or multiple copies of this article are available for a fee from The Haworth Document Delivery Service [1-800-HAWORTH, 9:00 a.m. - 5:00 p.m. (EST). E-mail address: docdelivery@haworthpress.com].

doi:10.1300/J120v45n93_04

represents new opportunities and challenges. Music librarians are being called upon to provide services to patrons they may never see. *[Article copies available for a fee from The Haworth Document Delivery Service: 1-800-HAWORTH. E-mail address: <docdelivery@haworthpress.com> Website: <http://www.HaworthPress.com> © 2006 by The Haworth Press, Inc. All rights reserved.]*

**KEYWORDS.** Music libraries, music reference, reference sources, user demands, changes in user populations, changes in access

Contemporary libraries are marked by change. Common examples of change include the exchange of card catalogs for their electronic counterparts, the change from one automated system to another, and the general move toward automating more library services. These changes present opportunities for more efficient library use by patrons and more efficient library services by staff. They can also present significant challenges.

Music collections are not exempt from the changes that are affecting the rest of the library community. Music users, like general users, come from a variety of backgrounds, and have varying comfort levels with technology. Because many music libraries serve academic communities, which are by nature characterized by the turnover of student bodies, the challenge of change may be greater for the librarian than for some patrons. This, however, may only be with respect to familiarity and comfort with the use of computer technology. Patrons may have difficulty understanding concepts of the library that are common to music collections, such as uniform titles and music subject headings. Patrons' comfort with computers coupled with the widespread use of computers to access library catalogs and other databases may create a false sense of ability. This is particularly true if patrons do not understand the intricacies of the organization of music materials in a library catalog.

The climate of change in music reference represents a challenge to librarians. The three issues that probably have had the greatest impact on reference service are changes in users, sources, and modes of access to sources. These three issues are certainly related, as users need to use sources, and they need to know how to access them in order to use them. Music libraries have their own peculiarities, however. Because they contain a wider variety of materials than many other kinds of library collections, reference librarians for music collections must be aware of the format, content, and intended uses of these materials, as well as the research patterns of their patrons. In the recent past, as cultural norms have been challenged by the changing paradigm of Western culture, users have wanted to use music libraries in new ways and librarians should accommodate them. The musical genres used and requested by today's library patrons are different than they once were, both for listening and for academic study. A plethora of new reference sources are available to today's users and librarians. Many musical reference sources are now issued in electronic formats, challenging some users. The most important aspect of the use of electronic resources in music reference is the way they impact users.

Electronic delivery of information has opened many doors in music reference. Using utilities such as OCLC, patrons can gain access to music information from many places that would otherwise be inaccessible. Now that Internet usage has become widespread in libraries and library consortia have become commonplace, collections no longer need to attempt to encompass every item of potential interest to users. Interlibrary loan has become an easier, more streamlined process. As a result, librarians may need to provide services to patrons they never see. These patrons may be close or they may live far away. This change has implications for reference. Should reference librarians become involved in learning the listening and studying preferences of new populations? They may have to do this in order to justify their services. Music libraries are called to adapt in response to cultural change.

If libraries fail to address these changes in ways that encourage the use of the collections, they will cease to be relevant. This essay illustrates the main areas of change in music collections, as they are presented in the library literature.

## USERS ARE CHANGING

Librarians should not assume that the service provided to users of music libraries decades ago would be adequate today. Users are demanding different kinds of music and literature on music from today's music libraries. In decades past, libraries could serve the user population by providing a collection of Western art music, related literature, and a reference librarian trained in the Western music tradition. Collection emphases are changing in response to demand from users. While the Western music tradition continues to be the backbone of many music library collections, this is changing as the needs of users change. New populations are now being served by music collections.[1] As the user base changes, along with sources and modes of access, reference service to music collections often must involve an instructional component. This is because new users are probably unfamiliar with the way music and music information is organized in a library.

### Users Are Demanding Broader Subject Coverage

One of the characteristics of the populations now being served by music collections is a desire to play and listen to music outside of the Western art tradition and also to read about such music. Librarians can best serve these users by developing their collections to include music from outside the Western art tradition and becoming familiar with these varieties of music. While the ability to use reference sources and teach patrons how to use them is a hallmark of the professional reference librarian, nothing can replace personal knowledge. Fortunately, many, many new publications are being issued each year that address music outside the Western art tradition. Familiarity with these publications and with the varieties of music they represent will help the librarian provide adequate reference service. Two particular varieties of music that are being emphasized in collections currently are world music and popular music.

### Immigrants Are Demanding World Music Coverage

For the purposes of this essay, world music shall be understood to encompass all music that originated outside the influence of Western art music. The United States, as a nation composed largely of immigrants and their descendents, owes much of its musical heritage to foreign countries. The early European immigrants to the United States and their descendents shaped the preference for European culture in the United States. The teaching of music in academic institutions focused on Western art music as the ideal for much of the last century. Librarians in music collections often received their musical education in this tradition. D. W. Krummel addressed this phenomenon at the International Association of Music Libraries, Archives, and Documentation Centres Annual Conference in 1982 in Brussels. In his report on the status of education for music librarians, he cautioned, "Music librarians are over-trained as musicians when the training produces high standards that amount to a constraint."[2] Krummel was referring specifically to standards associated with training in the Western art music tradition.

Large numbers of immigrants are still entering the United States, but they are overwhelmingly not coming from European countries.[3] Jeanette Casey and Kathryn Taylor report, "in 1950, . . . America was still the great melting pot and people were expected to share in American ideals and values, which included the idea that Western European classical music was the 'best' music."[4] Casey and Taylor attribute the lessening of these expectations to the multiculturalism that emerged from the societal changes of the 1960s.[5] Because music collections now serve a multicultural society, both in the public library and in the academic library, they should be developed to include the music demanded by society. Users who are immigrants or live in ethnic communities in diaspora may have a desire to use music materials that reflect their culture. Also, academic collections should be developed to support programs in ethnomusicology where appropriate.

## Many Users Are Demanding Popular Music Coverage

The proliferation of popular music in recent decades has spread to demands on music collections. Users not only want to listen to popular music, increasingly, they want to study it as an academic subject. Scholarly works on popular music are being published at an increasing rate, and evidence suggests that this trend will continue for the foreseeable future.[6] Casey and Taylor report that music library patrons at the Chicago Public Library are increasingly asking for popular music.[7] Librarians who are in touch with this trend can effectively plan services that address patrons' needs. Clearly, this has implications for collection development, but it also has implications for reference service. Librarians who have a working knowledge of popular music and popular music scholarship are and will continue to be equipped to provide service to this growing demand from patrons.

## New Populations Are Being Served

As music collections grow in non-Western countries, people in those countries will be exposed to new varieties of music. This will undoubtedly be helped by the proliferation of electronic union catalogs, such as OCLC's WorldCat. John Druesedow predicts that coverage of Western art music may be demanded in the future in libraries of non-Western countries.[8] Whether or not Western art music becomes a demand in non-Western countries, librarians should keep in mind the potential of electronic access to library materials as a means to serve new populations.

## *MUSIC REFERENCE SERVICE*
## *OFTEN LEADS TO INSTRUCTION*

The complex nature of music reference often puts users in the position of needing instruction to find and use the information they seek efficiently. Users who are interested in vocal works may need instruction in the sources that provide access to songs and arias in collections. Indexes to popular music collections and discographies may be cumbersome for novice users, so the reference librarian may be called upon to provide instruction. Uniform titles may baffle many novice users, but instruction could show them that they can also be powerful tools. In each of these cases, librarians could provide reference services that would generate satisfactory answers to patron requests, but reference alone would not necessarily enable the patron to develop the information literacy required for independent library use. Some music librarians, particularly in academic libraries, provide class or small group instruction in the use of music collections. These sessions only partially satisfy the need for instruction. David Lasocki comments, "Everyone pays lip service to the need for bibliographic instruction, but the task is mammoth. Meanwhile, we do a great deal of instruction, one-on-one, at the reference desk."[9] The reference librarian must exercise judgment when deciding to provide instruction as part of a reference encounter. Many factors may influence the appropriateness of such instruction. For example, the faculty member in the school of music who needs a reference to a song in a collection for a rehearsal that begins in five minutes will probably not be receptive to an on-the-spot instruction session. In this case, in the interest of good public relations, the librarian is called upon to provide efficient, accurate service.

## *SOURCES ARE CHANGING*

The body of material present in today's music reference collections has changed considerably over the past couple of decades. These changes reflect many of the demands of music library users. Among these are greater coverage of world music topics and popular music topics.[10] These are by no means the only changes that have occurred and will no doubt continue to occur in music reference collections. Publishers are issuing works with better indexes, probably at least partly due to demand from music librarians. New technologies are changing the way sources are presented. As online delivery of content is becoming more affordable, publishers are beginning to offer their content online, replacing CD-ROM and print formats. This is opening up some interesting possibilities, such as the online delivery of sound files connected with reference works. Librarians will need to watch these trends carefully in order to keep abreast of them and provide effective service to patrons.

## The Quality of Sources Is Improving

Addressing the 1986 Conference on Music Bibliography at Northwestern University, Ann Basart reported the needs perceived by librarians who participated in two surveys she conducted in 1982 and 1986.[11] Included in her report were the needs for retrospective indexing of music periodicals and online delivery of music periodical indexes.[12] In addition, she reported several concerns about the state of *The New Grove Dictionary of Music and Musicians:*

> Next to periodical indexing, my respondents were most concerned with *The New Grove*. A number of people said that they wanted an effective index to the work. . . . Others suggested that *The New Grove* should be available on CD-ROM, for full-text searching, which would obviate the problem of producing a comprehensive index.[13]

In addition to Basart's report, the Subcommittee on Bibliographic Standards for Reference Works of the Music Library Association's Reference and Public Services Committee issued a list of principles to guide publishers and writers of reference works in music in 1994.[14] Guideline 4.13 of that work states (in reference to the general organization of reference works), "Provide multiple means of access" (e.g., indexes, cross-references, table of contents).[15] Further, guideline 30.2 of the work states (in reference to the organization of dictionaries and encyclopedias), "Include indexes, especially in multi-volume sources with lengthy articles. Indexes can help reduce the number of cross-references."[16] The implementation of these guidelines in reference works would improve their ease of use thus improving the quality of the services of the library.

The publication of the reference gaps in Basart's article and the Music Library Association guidelines may indeed have had an effect on the publishers of reference works, particularly *The New Grove* and periodical indexes. In 2001, *The New Grove* was issued in its second edition, with an index, in print and in an online version. The online version also has the capability to include sound files with the articles. This is a new offering, requiring the free Sibelius Scorch browser plug-in; it promises to bring new depth to the content of *The New Grove*. A CD-ROM version of *The New Grove* was not issued, but online delivery has surpassed the need for such a version. Publishers of periodical indexes in music have made tremendous strides. In particular, *The Music Index* and *RILM Abstracts of Music Literature* are now available via online delivery, and the appearance of the *International Index to Music Periodicals* in 1996 has provided retrospective indexing of many periodicals to 1874. Librarians should request and watch for similar improvements in the music reference literature.

### Reference Sources Are Being Issued in Electronic Formats

Some reference sources are particularly suited to the electronic environment. It may go without saying that periodical indexes can be greatly improved by making them available online. Searches that would take a skilled researcher an afternoon to complete may now be completed in a matter of minutes. Also, the potential for searching by access points other than subject and author is made available with electronic indexes. Sources that require constant updates may be most effective in electronic form. A morbid but appropriate example of such a source is "Necrology" on the Web site of the Gaylord Music Library of Washington University in St. Louis.[17] This site, reporting the deaths of musical figures, is updated daily. The frequency of updates required to keep this site current suggests that electronic delivery is the best way to publish its content. The fifth edition of *Music Reference and Research Materials* by Vincent Duckles and Ida Reed contains an entire chapter on electronic reference sources.[18] Many new reference sources have become available online since the publication of the latest edition of *Music Reference and Research Materials*. One such electronic source is "DW3 Classical Music Resources," which claims to be "the world's most comprehensive collection of classical music links."[19] This Web site was launched in September 1999, and provides a valuable service to the world of music information as a noncommercial Web resource indexing music Web sites with multiple access points.[20] The proliferation of such publications will require librarians to become familiar with them and to develop strategies for introducing them to music library users.

### Changes in Sources Reflect Changes in Users

As the demographics of music library users have changed, so has the availability of reference works on a variety of topics in music. In addition to the availability of *The Garland Encyclopedia of World Music* and *The Encyclopedia of Popular Music*, many other sources are available providing coverage to a multiplicity of subjects in ways not previously covered in music reference collections. Some new reference sources cover such diverse topics as women musicians in the United States,[21] Tin Pan Alley Song,[22] and contemporary Christian music.[23] These sources represent a trend of new works published to fill reference needs in music libraries. The library community would be well served by the continued publication of new reference works.

Music users would benefit greatly from indexes to the programs of major orchestras and opera companies. The "Cleveland Orchestra Program Notes Index" is a good example of this kind of publication.[24] Because it is delivered over the World Wide Web, this source can be continually updated. Researchers can locate particular performances of works and gain access to the applicable program notes in collected sets of programs. As new works become available, librarians should take the time to familiarize themselves with these publications. Users of music collections can benefit from these sources as new means of locating the music they want along with information about the music.

Another related concern has to do with the changing format of sound recordings. Every time a new format for recorded sound becomes an accepted standard, libraries must meet the needs of housing and providing access to these recordings. The advent of the compact disc in the 1980s resulted in the purchasing by libraries of shelving and playback equipment for the new format. If, or more likely when, a computer file format becomes the accepted standard for recorded sound, this will present a new set of challenges for the music librarian. Server space will need to be dedicated for the sound recording collection, and the librarian will need to become familiar with the playback issues of this format. Another alternative would be a subscription arrangement with a service provider of recorded sound files. The forward-thinking librarian may also expect some patrons to be confused by the electronic delivery of yet another aspect of the library's collection.

## MODES OF ACCESS ARE CHANGING

As technological advances continue to bring about changes in library catalogs and databases, librarians must continue to learn how to use the newest versions of these. Patrons may feel uncomfortable using new technologies. This author has encountered users in his library attempting to perform searches for current books and printed music on the card catalog, even though the sign attached to it informs users that the catalog only covers sound recordings and that it has not been updated since 1982! This illustrates the need for librarians to develop an awareness of the observable research patterns of their patrons. The reference librarian can offer to help people perform searches for music on computerized catalogs and databases. Reference librarians who work with music collections should understand and be able to provide instruction in efficient music searching, especially for searches in which there is not a known item. Controlled vocabularies for description and access must be understood. Music uniform titles can be confusing, but their potential for locating items is immense. Patrons should be instructed whenever possible in their use and their purpose. Librarians should also take the time to understand and communicate the best ways to search online periodical indexes and other databases. Frequently these databases have their own controlled vocabularies, and patrons would do well to understand how these work.

### New Catalog Systems Are Being Developed

Most reference librarians are probably at least fundamentally familiar with the ubiquitous MARC format and the second edition of the Anglo-American Cataloging Rules as standards for description of and access to library materials. However, many may not be familiar with how these standards are put to work in the variety of online catalog systems available today. Reference librarians should watch how controlled vocabularies are displayed in the online catalog and they should make sure that they are usable to their full extent. The way uniform titles and subject headings display in online catalogs can have a major effect on the efficiency of a search for music materials. Richard Smiraglia identified four functions for uniform titles. The first of these is, "to draw together in the catalog bibliographic descriptions of various physical manifestations of a particular work. . . . "[25] When library catalogs provide hypertext enrichment for uniform titles, they accomplish Smiraglia's purpose for the user. A click on the title will bring up all the associated bibliographic records, sometimes simplifying a more complex search. Catalog searching can be very efficient when the system can generate a browsable list of all the bibliographic records that contain a particular uniform title. The same is true of subject headings. Another concern is the proper display of the format of music materials. Jane Gottlieb cautions:

> Automated library catalogs must display information on musical works in a manner that clearly distinguishes the format of the material (scores from sound recordings; vocal scores from full scores; large-sized full scores from miniature scores, etc.) and allow users to efficiently select from what may be dozens of different manifestations of Beethoven's *Archduke Trio* or hundreds of different manifestations of his *Eroica Symphony (No. 3, op. 55, E[-flat] major)*.[26]

Often these different formats are kept in different locations. If users know this, they can proceed to the items they desire, and often the online catalog is the only way they will know where to look. Technological advances and user dissatisfaction are two reasons why some libraries may choose to adopt new catalog systems. It is up to the music reference librarian then to learn the use of these systems and communicate with the parties responsible for local configuration so that the most optimal configuration can be set.

### Periodical Indexes Are Widely Available Online

All three major periodical indexes in music, *RILM*, *The Music Index*, and the *International Index to Music Periodicals*, are available online. As Basart suggested, this is a desired improvement.[27] Many of the same problems encountered with online catalogs are also present in online periodical indexes. For example, these indexes use controlled vocabularies, but these are frequently not the same controlled vocabularies used in the library catalog. Therefore, the librarian must be familiar with the use of these vocabularies and be able to communicate their use to music library patrons.

The online availability of these databases has many advantages. Depending on licensing agreements, libraries can make these databases available to users connecting via the Internet from offsite locations. Now university music students can do a large portion of their research from the comfort of their residence halls or apartments. Professors can connect from their offices or homes. These advantages for access carry potential challenges for reference and instruction. Users may not ask for help if they are having difficulty using these resources from remote locations. Librarians can address this problem by developing an online presence in the form of online (e-mail or chat) reference service and instructional services (online tutorials).

### More Periodical Indexes Are Available in Music

The introduction of the *International Index to Music Periodicals* in 1996 as the third major periodical index in music was a watershed moment in music librarianship. Now, librarians have three indexes from which to choose. This has implications for serials budgets as well as reference. Institutions with limited budgets are forced to decide which indexes are worth purchasing. Librarians at institutions with large enough budgets to afford *RILM*, *The Music Index*, and the *International Index to Music Periodicals* must decide which indexes to recommend to their patrons for specific needs. Leslie Troutman and Alan Green have both recently written comparatively about the quality of these indexes.[28] These contributions to the literature highlight the timeliness and importance of this issue. In addition, both *RILM* and *The Music Index* are still being published in cumulative print volumes. Librarians are now being faced with decisions about which publications to keep, and which versions of which publications to keep.

### CONCLUSION

As with many areas of contemporary librarianship, the tools, techniques, and service populations of music reference are subject to change over time. Librarians must respond to the climate of change proactively to deliver the most optimal services to their users. If librarians fail to respond in this way, services to patrons will suffer. If patrons perceive services as inadequate, they will come to the library for their music needs more and more infrequently, and the music collection will cease to be relevant. As outlined in this paper, significant changes have been reported in user populations; therefore librarians often must address cultural differences between themselves and patrons. Reference sources have undergone many improvements, including the inclusion of indexes in newer editions, as in the second edition of *The New Grove*. New reference sources are covering a wider spectrum of musical topics. Widespread availability of online periodical indexes has greatly improved potential access to music articles, but each index has its problems. E-mail and chat-based reference service and online instructional services continue to expand the reach of the music reference librarian, when they are used. Some librarians may be reluctant to accept or respond to the climate of change in favor of continuing traditionally accepted subject coverage and modes of access. This position, however, is likely to lead to unsatisfactory reference encounters if patrons desire access to new kinds of coverage and technology.

Fortunately for proactive librarians, many opportunities exist for keeping abreast of change, such as professional e-mail discussion lists, journals, and professional conferences. Librarians with music reference responsibilities would be well advised to take advantage of these opportunities. However, perhaps the most direct, if occasionally cryptic opportunities are reference encounters. Library patrons are possibly the librarian's best indicator of change. They supply the librarian with a wealth of knowledge about what they want every time an encounter occurs. The progressive librarian can assess patrons' needs and develop services to meet them. Finally, once effective services are developed, sharing new knowledge is incumbent upon the librarian through established channels of professional communication.

## NOTES

1. An example of this is presented by Jeanette Casey and Kathryn Taylor as they describe changes in patrons who use the music collection at the Chicago Public Library in "Music Library Users: Who Are These People and What Do They Want from Us?" *Music Reference Services Quarterly* 3, no. 3 (1995): 7. They describe a trend in user preference for popular music and the music of immigrants' countries of origin, often not Western countries.

2. Krummel, D. W. "Kindeldey Revisited: American Music Library Education in 1937 and 1982," *Fontes Artis Musicae* 30 (January-June 1983): 59.

3. 1,063,732 immigrants entered the United States in 2002, 1,064,318 entered in 2001, and 849,807 entered in 2000. The only European countries of birth among the top twenty countries of birth in each of these years were Bosnia-Herzegovina, Ukraine, Russia, and the United Kingdom. The remaining countries of birth in the top twenty in 2002, which were not European, accounted for 61.7 percent of the total immigrant pop-

ulation. U.S. Department of Homeland Security, *Yearbook of Immigration Statistics, 2002*. Washington DC: U.S. Government Printing Office, 2003, 8, table B. Available from http://www.immigration.gov/graphics/shared/aboutus/statistics/Yearbook2002.pdf. Accessed 21 October 2003.

4. Casey and Taylor, "Music Library Users," 6.

5. Ibid., 6-7.

6. To gauge the rise in the publication of books addressing popular music by university presses, this author performed searches of OCLC's *WorldCat* and Bowker's *Books in Print* on 19 September and 21 September 2003. In each database, he specified "popular music" in the subject field and "university" in the publisher field, excluded fiction, and limited each search to several five-year increments. In *Books in Print*, he included out-of-print titles. From 1984-1988, he found 15 books in *Books in Print* and 50 books in *WorldCat*. From 1989-1993, he found 56 books in *Books in Print* and 83 books in *WorldCat*. From 1994-1998, he found 107 books in *Books in Print* and 87 books in *WorldCat*. Finally, from 1999-2003, he found 104 books in *Books in Print* and 119 books in *WorldCat*.

7. Casey and Taylor, "Music Library Users," 7.

8. Druesedow, John E. "Reference Sources," *Notes: Quarterly Journal of the Music Library Association* 56 (March 2000): 619.

9. Lasocki, David. "Reference," *Notes: Quarterly Journal of the Music Library Association* 56 (March 2000): 607.

10. Prime examples of reference works in these areas include Ruth M. Stone, ed., *The Garland Encyclopedia of World Music*. New York: Garland, 1998, 10 vols.; and Colin Larkin, comp. and ed., *The Encyclopedia of Popular Music*, 3rd ed. London: MUZE UK, 1998, 8 vols. (appearing in previous editions as *The Guinness Encyclopedia of Popular Music*).

11. Basart, Ann. "Reference Lacunae: Results of an Informal Survey of What Librarians Want," *Music Reference Services Quarterly* 2, no. 3/4 (1993): 365-84.

12. Ibid., 366.

13. Ibid., 367.

14. Hunter, David et al. "Music Library Association Guidelines for the Preparation of Music Reference Works," *Notes: Quarterly Journal of the Music Library Association* 50 (June 1994): 1329-38.

15. Ibid., 1331.

16. Ibid., 1336.

17. Available at http://library.wustl.edu/units/music/necro/, viewed 21 October 2003.

18. See chapter 12 in Vincent H. Duckles and Ida Reed, *Music Reference and Research Materials: An Annotated Bibliography*, 5th ed. (New York: Schirmer, 1997), 613-22. Citations from this chapter are available online at http://www2.lib.ukans.edu/musiclib/duckles.htm. Accessed 21 October 2003.

19. Available at http://www.lib.duke.edu/music/resources/classical_index.html. Accessed 21 October 2003.

20. Fineman, Yale. "DW3 Classical Music Resources: Managing Mozart on the Web," *Portal: Libraries and the Academy* 1 (October 2001): 384-85.

21. Burns, Kristine H., ed. *Women and Music in America Since 1900*. Westport, CT: Greenwood, 2002.

22. Hinschak, Thomas S. *The Tin Pan Alley Song Encyclopedia*. Westport, CT: Greenwood, 2002; and Ken Bloom, *American Song: The Complete Companion to Tin Pan Alley Song*. New York: Schirmer, 2001, vols. 3-4.

23. Powell, Mark Allan. *Encyclopedia of Contemporary Christian Music*. Peabody, MA: Hendrickson, 2002. This publication was issued with an accompanying CD-ROM with the complete, searchable text of the work and links to Web sites of featured musicians.

24. Available from http://www.cim.edu/libProgNotes.php. Accessed 21 October 2003.

25. Smiraglia, Richard. *Describing Music Materials*, 3d ed., rev. and enl. with Taras Pavlovsky. Lake Crystal, MN: Soldier Creek Press, 1997, 171.

26. Gottlieb, Jane. "Reference Service for Performing Musicians: Understanding and Meeting Their Needs," *The Reference Librarian*, no. 47 (1994): 51.

27. Basart, "Reference Lacunae," 365-66.

28. Troutman, Leslie. "Comprehensiveness of Indexing in Three Music Periodical Index Databases," *Music Reference Services Quarterly* 8, no. 1 (2001): 39-51; and Green, Alan. "Keeping Up with the Times: Evaluating Currency of Indexing, Language Coverage and Subject Area Coverage in the Three Music Periodical Index Databases," *Music Reference Services Quarterly* 8, no. 1 (2001): 53-68.

# A Primer on Copyright Law
# and the DMCA

Byron Anderson

**SUMMARY.** Presents the basics of modern copyright law and ways in which the 1998 Digital Millennium Copyright Act (DMCA) changed the law. Focuses on the DMCA's prohibition of circumvention and file sharing and how this has impacted libraries. Discusses efforts to re-establish a copyright balance between creators, publishers and consumers, especially through proposed legislation and the open access movement. The impact of the DMCA on libraries is weighed, and calls for librarians to be more vigilant in opposing efforts to legalize digital rights management software. *[Article copies available for a fee from The Haworth Document Delivery Service: 1-800-HAWORTH. E-mail address: <docdelivery@haworthpress.com> Website: <http://www.HaworthPress.com> © 2006 by The Haworth Press, Inc. All rights reserved.]*

**KEYWORDS.** Copyright law, copyright legislation, Digital Millennium Copyright Act, circumvention, file sharing, open access journals, digital rights management software

---

Byron Anderson is Head of Reference, University Libraries, Northern Illinois University, DeKalb, IL 60115 (E-mail: banderson@niu.edu).

[Haworth co-indexing entry note]: "A Primer on Copyright Law and the DMCA." Anderson, Byron. Co-published simultaneously in *The Reference Librarian* (The Haworth Information Press, an imprint of The Haworth Press, Inc.) No. 93, 2006, pp. 59-71; and: *New Directions in Reference* (ed: Byron Anderson, and Paul T. Webb) The Haworth Information Press, an imprint of The Haworth Press, Inc., 2006, pp. 59-71. Single or multiple copies of this article are available for a fee from The Haworth Document Delivery Service [1-800-HAWORTH, 9:00 a.m. - 5:00 p.m. (EST). E-mail address: docdelivery@haworthpress.com].

## INTRODUCTION

Copyright laws shape libraries. Copyright principles, particularly first sale and fair use, are legal cornerstones of library services. The principle of first sale allows libraries to purchase works and loan them to patrons. The principle of fair use grants certain rights to users of copyrighted material to copy, download, and transfer files. Section 107 of the Copyright Law states that the reproduction of a work "for purposes such as criticism, comment, news reporting, teaching (including multiple copies for classroom use), scholarship, or research, is not an infringement of copyright" (U.S. Copyright Office, 2003). Section 108 of the law grants limited exclusive rights to libraries and archives to reproduce a copy of a work.

For roughly two centuries, time-honored user rights have helped stimulate free inquiry that, in turn, have stimulated new products, new ideas, and new knowledge. At the same time, authors and creators are granted certain rights in order to ensure an adequate return for their efforts. In the U.S. Constitution, Article I, Section 8, Clause 8, Congress grants the power "To promote the progress of science and the useful arts, by securing for limited times to authors and inventors the exclusive right to their respective writings and discoveries." United States copyright law, carefully crafted from George Washington's call for Congress to pass a copyright act in 1790, is a meticulous attempt to balance the interests of producers and users. The rights of authors and inventors were established initially at fourteen years with the option of renewing for another fourteen years. Congress has gradually extended the length of copyright to the current life of the author plus seventy years (or for a joint work, life of the last surviving author plus seventy years) for all works created on or after January 1, 1978. For works created before this period see Length of Copyright Terms, http://www2.tltc.ttu.edu/Cochran/length_of_copyright_terms.htm. A third group, publishers, have legal rights by transfer. Authors transfer rights to publishers in order to bring their works to market. A crucial function of the Copyright Act is to help equalize the bargaining language among the three groups: creators, publishers, and consumers, including libraries.

A lot is at stake in the copyright law. For the past twenty years, the copyright industry has grown almost three times as fast as the economy as a whole, according to the International Intellectual Property Alliance, a trade group representing film studios, book publishers, and other media (Mann, 1998). Copyrighted material is among the most prominent and lucrative of exports in the United States. Copyright is seen as a key to wealth in the digital age, and billions of dollars are at stake. Yet, with the capability of mass distribution comes mass abuse. Laws preventing this abuse greatly affect copyright users.

## COPYRIGHT BASICS

Copyright provisions are written into federal law based on many court cases over an extended period of time. The courts have developed four factors to evaluate and balance fair use cases remembered by Mary Minow's PNAM memory trick–Purpose, Nature, Amount, Market (2003). These four factors focus on circumstantial facts used in determining fair use of copyrighted works:

- The purpose and character of the use, whether such use is of a commercial nature or is for nonprofit educational purposes. Courts generally weigh in favor of nonprofit educational purposes, and if use is to create a new work with a different purpose.
- The nature of the copyrighted work. Use of nonfiction is generally weighed more favorably than works of fiction, poetry and art.
- The amount and substantiality of the portion used in relation to the copyrighted work as a whole. The smaller the amount copied the better, and the portion used is not the heart of the work.
- The effect of the use upon the potential market for or value of the copyrighted work. A work will either need to be shown as not having a significant effect on the market for the original work or does not deprive the creator of income.

For a more complete focus on factual circumstances important to the evaluation of copyrighted works, see Kenneth Crews' "Fair Use Checklist: Introduction," http://www.iupui.edu/copyinfo/.

There are three instances in which copyright protection is granted that may surprise some users of materials, either in print or online. First, a work does not need to indicate copyright for an owner to receive protection, though it's a good idea for producers to have this on his or her work(s). Second, unpublished works fall under the domain of copyright and can include the heirs of an unpublished work. Third, most works on the Internet have copyright protection. In this instance, public domain of the digital world is not necessarily the same as public domain of the print world. In the print world, after the life of the author plus seventy years a work will pass into the public domain no longer protected by copyright law. On the other hand, "public domain" on the Web is largely made up of freely accessible material though most of it is under copyright protection. Use of this material is limited to copyright restrictions, generally based on the four factors above. Unless otherwise stated or known, it is best to assume that Internet files are under copyright protection. At the same time, the Internet, too, has material based on lapsed copyrights, for example, Project Gutenberg, http://promo.net/pg, Internet's oldest producer of free electronic books, and Library of America, http://www.loa.org, a publisher dedicated to preserving by reprinting classic works of America's greatest writers.

Copyright law is periodically updated by Congress, but occasionally a landmark piece of legislation is passed such as the 1976 Copyright Act. This Act established modern copyright law by finding a balance between creators, publishers, and consumers. Soon thereafter, technology, or more specifically the accelerated pace of information and media technology, began to upset the balance. The digital age presented new challenges to fundamental copyright principles. Specific provisions in the copyright law found it difficult to keep up with the grueling pace of computer power that tended to double approximately every eighteen months. More power means more applications and features generating new issues involving copyright, for example, peer-to-peer file sharing features. Even with the accelerated pace of the information age, litigation of copyright issues can take years to work their way through the judicial process, sometimes resulting in a change in the law or a new law.

Congress, in part, under pressure to address copyright abuses and potential abuses caused by the quickening pace of technology, passed another landmark piece of legislation, the 1998 Digital Millennium Copyright Act (DMCA), effective October 2000. Section 103 of the DMCA adds a new chapter 12 to Title 17 of the *United States Code.* Sub-section 1201 "implements the obligation to provide adequate and effective protection against circumvention of technological measures used by copyright owners to protect their works" (Digital Millennium Copyright Act, 1998). In applying the DMCA to date, the courts seem to have leaned in favor of the copyright owner. Carrie Russell, Copyright Specialist for the American Librarian Association states, "From the passage of the 1998 DMCA, to the introduction of bills in state legislatures, such as the Uniform Computer Information Transactions Act (UCITA), lawmakers have given copyright owners real teeth in enforcing their agendas in the digital realm" (2003). The role of libraries as a copyright consumer has narrowed due to new restrictions on copying, downloading and file sharing. Russell quotes Eben Moglen, Columbia University cyberlaw expert who said, "content providers are using DRM [Digital Rights Management software] not just to guard against piracy but to create 'an absolutely leak-proof pipe' for delivering digital content. In other words, to control tightly and exploit every use of their copyrighted material." Russell continues with a quote from Gary Shapiro, president and CEO of the Consumer Electronics Association, "The technology industry is revolutionizing our ability to access and use information. This revolution grinds to a stop if the content industry is allowed to dictate the products, functions, and features available to consumers."

Russell puts the issue right on the mark when she says, "Unfortunately, DRM does not distinguish among uses. Fair use and piracy are viewed the same" (2003). With DRM, content owners can control both how their content is used and how it is accessed. The idea of browsing before deciding to read a book is eliminated by some applications of DRM. Julie Cohen, law professor at Georgetown University has described this as a threat to the right to read and that it portends negative long-term implications for how our society will be able to access and interact with information (Russell, 2003).

The DMCA represented a turning point in copyright law. In passing the DMCA, Congress cut short the legal process commonly used in the formulation of a law. The DMCA passed with little public notice, attention or involvement. The accelerated passage of the DMCA was contrary to the spirit and past practice of legislation. The DMCA caused one librarian notable, Walt Crawford, to blast the act as "a law that subsumes the First Amendment in the name of intellectual property protection, under fair use and first-purchase rights, and encourages the intermediaries to treat consumers as thieves" (2002).

Opponents of the DMCA worry that the legislation will be used to stifle new technology, threaten access to information, and move our country towards a pay-per-use society. There is a cadre of Internet software and entertainment companies working to create pricing models that will "meter, monitor, and monetize" Internet usage. These pricing structures will render moot the Web's early promise of a free medium of exchange (Chester & Rosenfeld, 2003). The ALA Copyright Agenda states, "As Congress becomes increasingly sympathetic to content providers' complaints about the economic impact of computer piracy, we expect continued efforts to pursue database protection and to expand the control of copyright holders under the guise of digital rights management legislation" (American Library Association, 2003).

## DMCA AND CIRCUMVENTION

The DMCA, among other things, bans circumvention of technological locks guarding access to a copyrighted work, prohibiting both circumvention of access controls for lawful purposes and the manufacture and distribution of technologies that enabled circumvention for these lawful purposes. There are six exemptions to the prohibition (Digital Millennium Copyright Act, 1998) that became effective in 2000:

- Nonprofit library, archive and educational institutions are permitted to circumvent solely for the purpose of making a good faith determination as to whether they wish to obtain authorized access to the work;
- Reverse engineering permits both circumvention and the development of technological means for such circumvention, by a person who has lawfully obtained a right to use a copy of a computer program for the sole purpose of identifying and analyzing elements of a program necessary to achieve interoperability with other programs, to the extent that such acts are permitted under copyright law;
- Encryption research permits circumvention of access control measures, and the development of the technological means to do so, in order to identify flaws and vulnerabilities of encryption technologies;
- Protection of minors allows a court applying the prohibition to a component or part to consider the necessity for its incorporation in technology that prevents access of minors to material on the Internet;
- Personal privacy permits circumvention when the technological measure, or the work it protects, is capable of collecting or disseminating personally identifying information about the online activities of a natural person;
- Security testing permits circumvention of access control measures, and the development of technological means for such circumvention, for the purpose of testing the security of a computer, computer system or computer network, with the authorization of its owner or operator.

Congress provided for a mandatory, periodic three-year review of the DMCA by the Register of Copyright and the Librarian of Congress to examine the applicability of an exemption. In the 2003 review, the Librarian of Congress recommended two additional exemptions and re-vised two other existing exemptions (Billington, 2003). First, a new exemption will allow those with a vision or print disability to circumvent technological protection measures in order to access literary works, including e-books, via a screen reader or text-to-speech or text-to-Braille device. Second, circumvention is allowed of computer software copy-protected by a media that is obsolete, including old games.

Modified exemptions from the 2003 review include software products, often known as "filtering software" or "blocking software," that restrict users from visiting certain Internet Web sites. These software products include compilations consisting of lists of Web sites to which the software will deny access. One application of this are filters that have been mandated by the Supreme Court in their recent ruling on the Children's Internet Protection Act (CIPA). The ruling requires libraries that receive federal funding to have filtering software on all public terminals; however, the exception permits circumvention of this software for the purposes of allowing adult library users upon request to access information that has been blocked. Librarians maintain that they must be able to determine which sites are being blocked so that they can assist adults who have a right to access a blocked site. Also modified is the exemption of computer programs protected by dongles that prevent access due to malfunction or damage and which are obsolete (Billington, 2003).

These exemptions are too narrow to prevent the DMCA from being invoked extensively to prevent circumvention and block distribution technologies. The DMCA Section 1201 does assure that the public will have the continued ability to make fair use of copyrighted works. At the same time, Section 1201 (c)(3) contains language clarifying that "the prohibition on circumvention devices does not require manufacturers of consumer electronics, telecommunication or computing equipment to design their products affirmatively to respond to any particular technological measure" (Digital Millennium Copyright Act, 1998). Hence, for example, the DeCSS decryption program, a file-sharing program that allows individuals to watch DVDs on a Linus-based computer, was made illegal under the DMCA. In addition, Section 1201(k) does mandate that within eighteen months of enactment of the DMCA, all analog videocassette recorders must be designed to conform to certain defined technologies, commonly known as Macrovision, currently in use for preventing unauthorized copying of analog videocassettes and certain analog signals. The provision prohibits right holders from applying these specified technologies to free television and basic and extended basic tier cable broadcasts. Without a change, the DMCA threatens to disenfranchise millions of Americans who want to copy from or transfer material among digital devices in the home.

## LEGAL ISSUES OF FILE SHARING

The courts have become legal battlegrounds for pundits for both intellectual freedom and intellectual property. Illegal use of file sharing is the single biggest abuse of digitized copyrighted material. For example, in Russia and China, more than 90 percent of all new business software is pirated (Mann, 1998). For online music, once a copyrighted song is downloaded, file-sharing software, such as Dazaa, Grokster, and Morpheus, automatically makes it available for other Internet users to download too. Online media analyst Big Champagne has estimated that more than 60 million Americans are using file-sharing software (Electronic Frontier Foundation, 2003). In an age of digitized manuscripts and scanners that can convert hard copy of digitized format, e-books, also, are clearly vulnerable to piracy. In their attempt to address abuses, a new bill was introduced in Congress by Reps. Howard Berman (D-CA) and John Conyers (D-MI) entitled, Author, Consumer, and Computer Owner Protection and Security Act of 2003 (HR 2752). The bill would make it a felony to upload even a single file of copyrighted material, and if passed, would cover most of the material on the Web.

Private organizations, such as the Recording Industry Association of America (RIAA), are trying to prevent file sharing by getting subpoenas targeting users, particularly college students, in the U.S. who are accused of being large-scale swappers of pirated music. The RIAA has not quantified what a "substantial amount" might be. Approximately seventy-five "fast-track" subpoenas–subpoenas that do not require the approval of a judge–were initially approved each day (MSN Entertainment Music News, 2003). In August 2003, Senator Norm Coleman (R-MN) opened an inquiry on whether RIAA's legal blitzkrieg was in violation of individual privacy rights. The RIAA plans to issue hundreds of additional subpoenas causing Coleman to question whether the DMCA is abusive. The number of lawsuits filed by October 1, 2003 was 261, though larger subpoena numbers are threatened by the RIAA. The effort by the RIAA to sue its way out of the current digital piracy dilemma was made possible by a recent federal court ruling under the DMCA. The ruling compelled Internet provider Verizon to hand over the name of an individual suspected of illegal file sharing on Verizon's network. Coleman does not question RIAA's need to fight piracy, but does question their tactics. An unintended consequence of the so-called P2P (peer-to-peer) wars is forcing university administrators to address the financial and manpower burdens of investigating DMCA violation notices. When a student is suspected of illegal file sharing, the service provider must investigate when notified. It's interesting to note that the service provider can be held liable, but not the software maker, in this case companies such as Grokster or Morpheus. Openly challenging these draconian measures by the RIAA is the Electronic Frontier Foundation's (EFF) "Let the Music Play" campaign launched in June 2003. EFF wants to find a better alternative that gets artists paid while making file sharing legal (Electronic Frontier Foundation, 2003).

Opponents of the DMCA are fighting back in an attempt to re-establish the balance between creators, publishers, and consumers. One method being employed is by introducing new legislation in favor of copyright consumers. For example, Representatives Rick Boucher (D-VA) and John Doolittle (R-CA) have introduced in Congress HR 107, the Digital Media Consumers' Rights Act of 2003. This bill reaffirms fair use in the digital environment by establishing a procedure in which the Federal Trade Commission will impose proper labeling requirements on the outside packaging, so consumers will know any limits on the recordability or playability of copy-protected CDs. Complementing this in the Senate is the Digital Consumer Right to Know Act, S 692, introduced by Senator Ron Wyden (D-OR). The American Library Association summary of the act states, "The purpose of the Act is to ensure that consumers of digital information and entertainment content are informed in advance of technological features that may restrict the uses and manipulation of such content" (American Library Association, 2003). These bills are viewed as an important first step in recognizing the rights of copyright users.

Building and broadening on HR 107 is HR 1066, the Benefit Authors without Limiting Advancement or Net Consumer Expectations (BALANCE) Act of 2003, introduced by Zoe Lofgren (D-CA). The bill proposes to protect fair use, allow first sale rights of digital content, and provides for permissible circumvention to enable fair use and consumer expectations. Rep. Lofgren also introduced in June 2003, HR 2601, the Public Domain Enhancement Act. The Act provides a mechanism to allow abandoned copyright works to pass into the public domain. The bill's introduction into Congress mentions a study indicating that only 2 percent of works between 55 and 75 years old continue to retain commercial value (Library of Congress, 2003). Under current law these abandoned works are unable to pass into public domain, preventing commercial and noncommercial entities from building upon, cultivating and preserving abandoned works. Many of these works could prove useful to the historian, artist or teacher. The Act requires that copyright owners pay a one-dollar fee fifty years after a copyrighted work has been published and every five years thereafter; otherwise, the work passes into the public domain. These bills are meant to signal Congress that copyright law must be re-calibrated to restore consumer and public rights.

## OPEN ACCESS MOVEMENT

Other ideas gaining momentum in helping re-establish copyright balance includes one that has gained a lot of support in the academic environment, the open access movement. Here, copyright owners waive some of the rights given by copyright law. This waiver would permit the unrestricted reading, downloading, copying, storing, printing, searching and linking of a work. Just as the DMCA prevents illegal circumvention of copyright protected systems, open access allows legal circumvention of copyright protected material via the author's waiver. Open access does not employ rights management software. Rather, it is about the sharing of knowledge, an idea supported by academics who give their consent because they write for impact not money. Open access as a funding model has a number of variables, but most focus on keeping prices low or free. In this manner, open access fights battles on several fronts: inflationary pricing in serials, closed distribution in high-priced databases, and monopoly control over journals, especially in STM (science, technology, medical) journals. Open access serves as an alternative to scholarly publication and is intricately involved in the debate with scholarly communication.

Open access projects have caught the attention of many academics, and significant among these projects is the Public Library of Science (PLoS), http://www.publiclibraryofscience.org. The PLoS is a nonprofit organization of scientists and physicians committed to making the world's scientific and medical literature a freely available public resource. Scientists generally want the maximum visibility for their research, and PLoS is designed to do this by allowing access in the public domain. Also worth mentioning is the Directory of Open Access Journals, http://www.doaj.org, a project that aims to increase the visibility and ease of use of open access scientific and scholarly journals thereby promoting increased usage and impact, and SPARC (Scholarly Publishing and Academic Resources Coalition), http://www.arl.org/sparc, "An alliance of universities, research libraries, and organizations built as a constructive response to market disfunctions in the scholarly communication system." Even Oxford University is experimenting with open access by placing one of its flagship journals, *Nucleic Acids Research*, in an open access environment. The journal's annual Database Issue is now freely available online at http://nar.oupjournals.org. If the experiment is successful, the rest of the journal will gradually move to the open access model.

A number of obstacles exist in the acceptance of the open access model. New business models need to be accepted because costs for electronic publishing do exist, that is, costs do not go away because something is placed in the public domain. Open access projects are moving toward either charging authors to publish–about $500 to $1500 per paper–or charging institutions a subscription fee which allows any of their researchers to subsequently publish free of charge (Owens, 2003). The "system pays" model works on the principle that the money for subscriptions comes from scientists' grants. Commercial publishers have countered that this fiscal model only shifts the cost internally within the institution and does not really address pricing, and that the "author pays" model is not economically viable for the long run. The conflict between open access publishing and commercial academic publishing is similar to the conflict between the recording industry and the free music files on Napster.

A second obstacle to acceptance of open access publications is that as long as scientists rely on publishing in high-impact journals to secure funding, there is no incentive to switch to open access models. A third obstacle is that open access publications have yet to achieve equal acceptance and status as print journals, and they're trying to do this within an institution known for a conservative pace of change. However, in the very first issue of a PLoS journal, PloS: Biology, http://biology.plosjournals.org, Duke University researcher Jose Carmena and others created a study that forced the world to take notice entitled, "Learning to Control a Brain-Machine Interface for Reaching and Grasping by Primates." Requiring that journals exercise peer-review or editorial quality control, such as those included in the Directory of Open Access Journals project, is a step in the right direction toward greater acceptance. Finally, society journals may find it difficult to move to an open access model because they rely on the profit from subscriptions to fund other activities.

Congressional legislation is moving in the same direction as the PLoS, and supported by PloS, particularly the Public Access to Science Act (2003), HR 2613, introduced by Representative Martin Olav Sabo (D-MN). This Act argues that U.S. residents shouldn't have to pay twice–one time with their tax dollars and a second time with subscription fees to scientific journals–for research that may improve their health or save their lives. The Act would amend the U.S. Copyright law so that copyright protection is not available for research "substantially funded" by the U.S. government. Without copyright protection, such research would be freely available in the public domain. The Act raises a number of questions and has its opponents. Current debate is asking at what level of federal funding would trigger the Sabo bill's copyright restrictions, and whether research partially funded by private organizations or other governments would be included (Gross, 2003). The Association of American Universities supports public access to federally-funded scientific research, but believes that the denial of copyright protection for publications resulting from federally-funded research is not only unnecessary but also may prove quite harmful to the nation's enterprise (American Association of University Presses, 2003).

## CONCLUSION

Copyright has become more complicated and is often caught in the middle of addressing other pressing issues such as online piracy, journals pricing, and scholarly communication. Clearly, there is a sense of urgency on the part of librarians to be vigilant and fight against those sections of the DMCA or features of DRM that threaten the mission of libraries. A proper perspective is called for in recognizing the rights of both the creator and user of protected information. Information and media technology should allow for fair use and first sale rights within the limits of the law. Libraries should be able to digitize works and users should be able to download, copy or send at least some acceptable portion of those works within defined limits of personal use. One new initiative, "middleware," uses a software layer that exists between the network and applications like DRM that could authenticate users, secure content, and ensure user privacy. It could also allow users to state their use requirements, for example, make a fair use copy. This is a practical application creating a practical solution. Many more initiatives are needed. Librarians cannot ignore the threat of digital rights management software and the legislation used to legalize it.

# REFERENCES

American Association of University Presses (2003). [Letter from N. Hasselmo, June 18]. Retrieved August 20, 2003 from http://www.aau.edu/intellect/Sabo7.18.03.pdf.

American Library Association, Office of Government Relations (2003). *2003 Copyright Agenda*. Retrieved February 12, 2004 from http://www.ala.org/ala/washoff/washevents/washannual2003/CopyrightAgenda2003.pdf.

Billington, J. (2003). Statement of the Librarian of Congress Relating to Section 1201 Rulemaking (October 28). Retrieved December 17, 2003 from http://www.copyright.gov/1201/docs/librarian_statement_01.html.

Chester, J. and Rosenfeld, S. (2003). *Stealing the Internet* (August 4). Retrieved August 11, 2003 from http://www.tompaine.comfeature2.cfm/ID/8528.

Crawford, W. (2002). The Crawford Files: Partnership, Properties, and Disintermediation. *American Libraries*, 33 (2), 59.

Electronic Frontier Foundation (2003). *'Let the Music Play' Campaign* (June 30). Retrieved August 13, 2003 from http://www.eff.org/IP/P2P/20030630_eff_pr.php.

Gross, G. Bill Seeks Free Access to Federally Funded Research (2003). *Bio-IT World News*, July 1. Retrieved August 4, 2003 from http://www.bio-itworld.com/news/070103_report2813.html.

Library of Congress (2003). *HR 2601* (June 23). Retrieved August 5, 2003 from http://thomas.loc.gov [type in Bill Number].

Mann, C. C. (1998). Who Will Own Your Next Good Idea? *Atlantic Monthly*, 282 (September), 57-82.

Minow, M. (2003). *How I Learned to Love Fair Use* (July 30). Retrieved August 14, 2003 from http://fairuse.stanford.edu/commentary_and_analysis/2003_07_minow.html.

Owens, S. (2003). Revolution or Evolution? *EMPO Reports* 4, 741-743.

Russell, C. (2003). Fair Use Under Fire. *Library Journal* (August 15) [Electronic version]. Retrieved August 29, 2003 from http://libraryjournal.reviewsnews.com/index.asp?layout=articlePrint&articleID=CA315183.

MSN Entertainment Music News (2003). *Tips for Music Fans to Avoid Net Trouble*, (July 28). Retrieved September 24, 2003 from http://entertainment.msn.com/news/article.aspx?news=129253.

U.S. Copyright Office (1998). *The Digital Millennium Copyright Act of 1998. U.S. Copyright Office Summary*. (December). Retrieved September 5, 2003 from http://www.loc.gov/copyright/legislation/dmca.pdf.

U.S. Copyright Office (2003). Copyright Law of the United States of America and Related Laws Contained in Title 17 of the *United States Code*. Section 107: *Limitations on exclusive rights: Fair use*. Retrieved September 5, 2003 from http://www.copyright.gov/title17/92chap1.html#107.

# Self-Service Interlibrary Loan:
# A Primer for Reference Staff

## Roberta Burk

**SUMMARY.** Technology is rapidly moving libraries toward a self-service interlibrary loan model. Patrons currently request books and articles through OCLC's unmediated ILL Direct Request service, and interlibrary loan management software enables users to request, track, and renew borrowed materials unassisted online. In addition, products such as SFX and Serials Solutions further expand unmediated requesting. Peer to peer resource sharing defined by the ISO ILL Protocol and direct consortial borrowing, which has become possible following the recently approved NCIP standard, encourage and support the widespread development of self-service interlibrary loan. As borrowing from other collections becomes an almost effortless process for library users, reference librarians must find ways to encourage patron use of local collections, as well as familiarize themselves with the mechanics of

Roberta Burk is Information Delivery Services Librarian, University Libraries, Northern Illinois University, DeKalb, IL 60115 (E-mail: rlburk@niu.edu).

[Haworth co-indexing entry note]: "Self-Service Interlibrary Loan: A Primer for Reference Staff." Burk, Roberta. Co-published simultaneously in *The Reference Librarian* (The Haworth Information Press, an imprint of The Haworth Press, Inc.) No. 93, 2006, pp. 73-82; and: *New Directions in Reference* (ed: Byron Anderson, and Paul T. Webb) The Haworth Information Press, an imprint of The Haworth Press, Inc., 2006, pp. 73-82. Single or multiple copies of this article are available for a fee from The Haworth Document Delivery Service [1-800-HAWORTH, 9:00 a.m. - 5:00 p.m. (EST). E-mail address: docdelivery@haworthpress.com].

unmediated interlibrary loan to better assist patrons in their use of evolving interlibrary loan technology. *[Article copies available for a fee from The Haworth Document Delivery Service: 1-800-HAWORTH. E-mail address: <docdelivery@haworthpress.com> Website: <http://www.HaworthPress.com>*

**KEYWORDS.** Academic libraries, unmediated interlibrary loan, NCIP (NISO Circulation Interchange Protocol), OCLC DirectRequest, direct consortial borrowing, interlibrary loan management software, ILL technology

## INTRODUCTION

Evolving technology continues to shape and reshape academic reference service. Professional journals and conferences remind us that virtual reference, information literacy, database licensing, and information portals are key issues facing reference librarians. Search committees charged with filling reference staff positions advertise for candidates expert in the use of electronic resources, digital reference initiatives, and electronic classrooms.

Reference librarians are well aware of the electronic revolution as it is affecting the reference service they provide, but they are much less likely to be familiar with the technology that is reshaping the processes that control resource sharing and document delivery. Information protocols and standards are ensuring a level of interoperability between new products that is steadily moving libraries toward what some are calling self-service interlibrary loan (Wanner, 2003). Yet familiarity with evolving interlibrary loan processes will become increasingly important to reference librarians as they find themselves guiding library users through the intersection of reference and interlibrary loan, where unmediated requesting of books and journal articles is transforming the way students and faculty conduct their research. Understanding the tools and techniques employed by academic interlibrary loan departments is useful for reference staff who work directly with students and faculty. Familiarity with interlibrary loan processes not only enables reference librarians to answer patron questions about obtaining material unavailable at the home library, but also alerts them to the ease with which library users are now able to request and receive material from outside sources, often without fully exploring their own library's collection.

## BACKGROUND

Traditionally, academic libraries have been proud of their collections and sought to provide materials, whether print or electronic, to support university curriculum and faculty research. Reference departments have existed to assist faculty and students in the use of resources provided by the library, ensuring maximum usage of the collection and the most immediate access for patrons. In those instances where needed material was not available in the local collection, the reference librarian most probably referred the student or faculty member to interlibrary loan and may have provided the patron with an interlibrary loan request form or directed him to an online request form available through the library's home page.

From this point of referral, however, the reference librarian was no longer part of the process. If the user had any question about the service, he was advised to speak to the interlibrary loan office. The interlibrary loan office, usually operating "behind-the-scenes," took the request form and created lender strings using one of the three major resource sharing utilities, OCLC, RLIN, or DOCLINE, to obtain the needed book or journal article, and later notified the patron of its arrival and answered any patron questions related to the process. The use of utility subsystems and their attendant lender strings, messaging files, and shipping mechanisms remained a mystery to most thankful reference librarians.

The relatively clear line that existed between reference and interlibrary loan became less clear when libraries began to join together to use shared online catalogs and circulation systems, enabling patrons to request books directly from other libraries within their consortium and thus bypassing the use of resource sharing utilities, as well as their library's interlibrary loan office. In the early 1990s, groups such as ILCSO, the Illinois Library Computer Systems Organization (Sloan, 1990) and OhioLINK (Prabha and O'Neill, 2001) were offering unmediated requesting to their patrons through the joint use of a shared catalog and patron database. With such unmediated requesting came less patron involvement with the interlibrary loan staff and more contact with the reference staff, who often assisted in the initial online catalog search for material. When that search produced citations for material not available locally, it was the reference librarian who could then instruct the patron in the mechanics of an unmediated request, and who would most likely be asked about interlibrary loan details such as when the book would arrive, where it should be picked up, and how it could be renewed. Still, the bulk of interlibrary loan transactions remained mediated, including those books not available through the shared consortial catalog and all journal article requests. Reference staff became adept at working with patrons and the shared catalog, but any transactions involving articles or materials from institutions outside the consortium were promptly referred to interlibrary loan.

## UNMEDIATED REQUESTING GROWS

OCLC introduced unmediated requesting of journal articles in 1997. Libraries using FirstSearch databases (including WorldCat) activate Direct Request service through the FirstSearch administrative module. Once Direct Request has been activated, patrons request material through an online request form linked to the bibliographic record of the desired article or book. The request form asks the user to supply patron information but not bibliographic information, which is automatically provided by the database. This not only simplifies the request process for users, but also ensures the submission of accurate citation information to the interlibrary loan office.

From this point, the library determines just how unmediated a process Direct Request will be. At its least automated, libraries choose the "Direct to Review File" option. This option directs all FirstSearch interlibrary loan requests to the OCLC Review File, where interlibrary loan staff look at each request and assign a lender string to the workform before sending the request out to the first of up to five potential lenders. Another possibility is the "Direct to Lender" option, which a library may choose if it wishes to ensure that all requests go out in a completely unmediated fashion and the library has no preferences concerning which libraries supply the material. If this option has been chosen, the patron submits his request from within the FirstSearch database and that request immediately goes out through OCLC to the first of any five libraries in the world who own the material. The third option, "Direct to Profile," allows libraries to create profiles (acting like filters) that direct the system to check for local ownership and that incorporate custom holdings into the DirectRequest process. Here library staff pre-determine groups of preferred lenders, such as libraries that have agreed to supply articles at no or low cost, libraries that are geographically close, or who have particularly short turnaround times, or meet whatever criteria the interlibrary loan staff ordinarily consider when determining which libraries to ask for a loan or photocopy. If the borrowing library has chosen this option, the user's request goes directly to the first of five libraries who match the "profile" already established, but if no libraries are found who match this profile, then the request is automatically sent to the OCLC Review File for staff intervention. This option allows routine requests to be filled in true unmediated fashion, while calling on the expertise of interlibrary loan staff to identify lenders for the more obscure materials.

## INTERLIBRARY LOAN MANAGEMENT SOFTWARE

Unmediated requesting has been further enhanced by interlibrary loan management software packages such as CLIO and ILLiad now used by many academic interlibrary loan departments. Such systems expand unmediated requesting to include the online interlibrary loan request forms most libraries provide. These forms are not linked to any particular database, such as the OCLC FirstSearch Direct Request forms; rather they allow users to request a known item, perhaps from a bibliography or instructor's suggested reading list, without linking to a bibliographic record first. While many libraries have provided their patrons with such online forms in the past, the submitted forms were generally routed to the home library's interlibrary loan office where they were printed out and handled manually. The ILL management software products now "harvest" these online requests as patrons submit them, automatically overlay an OCLC workform with the user-provided bibliographic information and patron-database provided user information, and if the library has selected either the "Direct to Lender" or "Direct to Profile" option, produce a request without any staff intervention. This feature of ILL management systems means that an even larger percentage of patron requests are unmediated and go out directly to potential lenders.

In addition to expanding unmediated requesting capabilities, ILL management products provide almost seamless delivery to patrons of articles sent to the library via Ariel. Ariel is Web-based delivery software that is used by over a thousand libraries worldwide to send and receive "photocopies." Articles are scanned by the lending library and sent via the Internet to the requesting library, where the articles are converted to PDF files and routed to a designated server at the library. To complete the process, an e-mail is automatically generated and sent to the patron with a link to the article on the server.

## *OpenURL LINKING AND INTERLIBRARY LOAN*

The development of products like SFX (Ex Libris, 2003) and Serials Solutions (Serials Solutions, 2003) which utilize OpenURL link resolvers to link digital content across various vendor databases has also meant an additional expansion of unmediated interlibrary loan. Designed to make it easier for patrons to get to full-text content across databases, these products also provide for a link to the library's online interlibrary loan request form. The link carries with it the citation information and automatically fills in the online request form accordingly. User information is supplied by the ILL management patron database record based on the user ID provided by the patron. In this unmediated scenario, the user searches one of the library's databases, which could be EBSCO, Ovid, FirstSearch, ProQuest, or any other, finds a citation to an article that interests him, sees that the content of the article is not available locally, either electronically or in print, and links to the ILL request form. Without manually entering any bibliographic or user information, the patron clicks a submit button and the article request goes out directly to a lending partner who scans and sends the requested article via Ariel. The article is routed to the library server, and the patron receives an e-mail linking him to the server and his requested article. The process is fast and easy, without interlibrary loan staff intervention at the patron's library.

## *UNMEDIATED REQUESTING BEYOND UTILITIES*

In the past, most libraries have relied on centralized-model utilities, such as OCLC, Docline or RLIN, to coordinate the interlibrary process. From the time requests were produced at the borrowing library, the utilities controlled the process; they monitored the request as it moved through a lender string and continued to track the borrowed item once a lender was found. Utilities made it possible for interlibrary loan staff to update item status from "filled" to "received," to "renewed," and finally to "returned." Referred to as "messaging," status updates have been an integral part of the process and relied on a central system to coordinate such communication between borrower and lender. FirstSearch Direct Request Service enhanced the OCLC model by adding patron-initiated unmediated functionality to the process, allowing patron requests to go directly to OCLC's centralized resource-sharing system. ILL management software (CLIO and ILLiad) completed the picture by providing an interface to OCLC that automates much of the messaging between libraries and creating a database that records borrowing and lending transactions enabling easier copyright reporting, borrowing and lending analysis, and billing capability. The basic system, however, remains a centralized one dependent upon OCLC to manage the requesting and lending process.

RLIN (Research Libraries Information Network), the other major utility, has recently embarked upon another approach. An information system developed by RLG (Research Library Group), RLIN has since 1975 provided its SHARES members, consisting of approximately 150 research libraries throughout the world, with a union catalog and a resource sharing mechanism similar to OCLC's centralized model. The RLIN ILL system was retired on August 31, 2003, and now operates in a peer-to-peer distributed interlibrary loan environment. RLIN ILL has been replaced by ILL Manager, interlibrary loan management software that utilizes an international standard known as the ISO ILL protocol to exchange requests with other systems, allowing them to go from the borrowing library directly to the lending library, bypassing completely a centralized utility and its attendant costs. ILL Manager, like ILLiad and CLIO, enables unmediated patron requesting, supports preferred-lender assignment and automated request routing, is fully integrated with Ariel, provides financial tracking and invoicing, and has the added advantage of free ILL messaging (Massie, 2000). Such institutions as the Library of Congress, Rutgers, and the University of Pennsylvania report successful implementation of peer-to-peer distributed interlibrary loan.

## NCIP (NISO CIRCULATION INTERCHANGE PROTOCOL) MOVES ILL TOWARD "DIRECT PATRON BORROWING" MODEL

Unmediated requesting and distributed resource sharing describe only part of the evolving interlibrary loan picture. In October 2002, the American National Standards Institute (ANSI) approved the Z39.83 protocol (National Information Standards Organization, 2002) developed by the National Information Standards Organization (NISO). Commonly referred to as NCIP (NISO Circulation Interchange Protocol), the new standard is now being incorporated into the circulation and interlibrary loan modules and related products of a number of vendors, including 3M, Auto-Graphics, Endeavor, epixtech, ExLibris, Fretwell-Downing, In-

novative Interfaces, OCLC, Relais, RLG, Sirsi, The Library Corpora-
tion and others (Jackson, 2002). NCIP-compliant circulation systems
will be able to communicate with compliant systems from other vendors
to facilitate direct interlibrary patron borrowing, including remote patron authentication, requesting, check-out, renewal, and check-in. Consortia such as ILCSO and OhioLink pioneered the "direct consortia
borrowing" model, but in order to work all members of the consortia
were required to use the same automated library system. NCIP makes
that same direct borrowing functionality available between libraries using independent library systems from different vendors as long as those
systems support the NCIP standard (Dorman, 2003), thus greatly expanding the opportunity for the development of innovative library partnerships and consortial arrangements.

Sometimes called "extended circulation," "self-service interlibrary
loan," "direct patron borrowing," or "direct consortial borrowing," the
new NCIP model includes circulation information in the interlibrary
loan transaction itself. ILL requests will be based on shelf status, not
simply on holdings; charged materials from other libraries will appear
on the user's circulation record, and renewal of those items will occur in
real time. The implementation and widespread use of NCIP-compliant
products promise considerable interlibrary loan cost savings and faster
service, as well. Early indications suggest that the cost of interlibrary
loan transactions could be reduced by as much as 75 percent when manually processed transactions are replaced by the direct consortia borrowing
model and the average turnaround time for requested monographs could
drop from an average of two weeks to as little as two days (Rogers,
2003).

## CONCLUSION

Simplifying interlibrary loan for users, getting borrowed materials to
them faster, and doing it more cheaply are the forces driving current ILL
innovation. Librarians must do everything possible to make access to
resource sharing as easy and seamless a process as possible, but not at
the expense of overlooking what is at hand. The more efficiently interlibrary loan operates, the more irresistible it becomes to users in need of
research materials. Perhaps more than ever before, reference librarians
must educate users through formal bibliographic instruction sessions
and through individual reference interviews to use local collections before turning to interlibrary loan to supply the first citations that appear in

a cursory database search. Too often these are not the best sources, but convenient ILL requesting may discourage the user from searching further. If the assignment calls for five references, the student clicks on the request button for the first five citations, and his research is finished for the day! The challenge facing reference librarians is to find ways to intercede in what is fast becoming self-service interlibrary loan.

Open communication between interlibrary offices and reference departments is essential, whether in the form of cross-training or regularly scheduled joint meetings where new interlibrary loan technologies and tools are shared. Not only would this help reference staff gauge the impact of emerging technology on patron research, but will also better qualify them to answer the inevitable questions concerning patron-initiated, unmediated, direct patron borrowing. Reference librarians become the logical source of help for patrons struggling to make the connection between the material they need and the technology that will get it for them.

# REFERENCES

Dorman, David. 2003. Technically Speaking: NCIP on the Move. *American Libraries* 34 (June/July): 104.

Ex Libris. 2003. Ex Libris, Forerunners of Change: SFX overview. Retrieved December 3, 2003 from http://www.aleph.co.il/sfx/index.html.

Jackson, Mary E. 2002. *Current Status of NCIP Implementations and ILL Policy Directory*. Paper presented at the 2002 American Library Association Annual Conference, Atlanta, Georgia, 15-18 June. Retrieved December 3, 2002 from http://www.ala.org/Content/NavigationMenu/RUSA/Our_Association2/RUSA_Sections/MOUSS/Our_Section4/Discussion_Groups7/Interlibrary_Loan3/NCIP.pdf.

Massie, Dennis R. 2000. RLG's ILL Manager: A Distributed Resource Sharing System for the New ISO ILL Environment or, How I Learned to Stop Worrying and Love International Standards. *Journal of Interlibrary Loan, Document Delivery & Information Supply* 11 (2): 23-37.

National Information Standards Organization. 2002. ANSI/NISO Z39.83-2002 Circulation Interchange part 1: Protocol (NCIP). Retrieved December 3, 2003 from http://www.niso.org/standards/standard_detail.cfm?std_id=728.

Prabha, Chandra G., and Edward T. O'Neill. 2001. Interlibrary Borrowing Initiated by Patrons: Some Characteristics of Books Requested via OhioLINK. *Journal of Library Administration* 34 (3/4): 329-338.

Rogers, Michael. 2003. Boston Library Consortium Launches NCIP ILL Service: New Offering Employs NISO Z39.83 Standard Through Dynix Universal Resource Sharing Application Tool. *Library Journal* 128 (May 1): 25.

Serials Solutions. 2003. Helping Librarians and Patrons Find and Use Their Full-text E-journals. Retrieved December 3, 2003 from http://SerialsSolutions.com.

Sloan, Bernard G. 1990. Future Directions for ILLINET Online. *Illinois Libraries* 72 (January): 40-44.

Wanner, Gail. 2003. *Is It Circulation or is It Interlibrary Loan? Benefits of Automating Interlibrary Loan Workflows Using the New NISO Z39.83 Standard.* Paper presented at the 8th Interlending and Document Supply International Conference, Canberra, Australia, 28-31 October. Retrieved December 3, 2003 from http://www. nla.gov.au/ilds/abstracts/isitcirculation.htm.

# From Novelty to Necessity:
# Impact of the PDA Experience
# on Medical Libraries

Peg Burnette
Jo Dorsch

**SUMMARY.** Handheld computers are quickly becoming a ubiquitous tool in medicine. Factors that have spurred the rapid adoption of this technology in medicine include convenience and ease of use, mobility, and the enormous library of medical applications now available. Health sciences libraries in both hospitals and academic medical centers are actively promoting and supporting PDAs as a natural extension of their services. Medical libraries have quickly adopted this technology to deliver medical information in a non-traditional way. This paper discusses approaches being used to incorporate PDAs into library services and examines the impact of those approaches on the medical reference librarian. *[Article copies available for a fee from The Haworth Document Delivery Service: 1-800-HAWORTH. E-mail address: <docdelivery@haworthpress.com> Website: <http://www.HaworthPress.com> © 2006 by The Haworth Press, Inc. All rights reserved.]*

Peg Burnette (E-mail: phburn@uic.edu) is Systems/Reference Librarian and Jo Dorsch (E-mail: jod@uic.edu) is Health Science Librarian, both at the Library of the Health Sciences-Peoria, University of Illinois College of Medicine at Chicago, Peoria, IL 61656 .

[Haworth co-indexing entry note]: "From Novelty to Necessity: Impact of the PDA Experience on Medical Libraries." Burnette, Peg, and Jo Dorsch. Co-published simultaneously in *The Reference Librarian* (The Haworth Information Press, an imprint of The Haworth Press, Inc.) No. 93, 2006, pp. 83-98; and: *New Directions in Reference* (ed: Byron Anderson, and Paul T. Webb) The Haworth Information Press, an imprint of The Haworth Press, Inc., 2006, pp. 83-98. Single or multiple copies of this article are available for a fee from The Haworth Document Delivery Service [1-800-HAWORTH, 9:00 a.m. - 5:00 p.m. (EST). E-mail address: docdelivery@haworthpress.com].

Available online at http://www.haworthpress.com/web/REF
© 2006 by The Haworth Press, Inc. All rights reserved.
doi:10.1300/J120v45n93_07

**KEYWORDS.** Personal Digital Assistant (PDA), handheld computing, handheld products, wireless access, medical reference, medical libraries, library services

## INTRODUCTION

PDA, personal digital assistant, palmtop, handheld computer, or by any other name, this small device has had a considerable impact on health sciences libraries in a short period of time. Health professionals, in particular, have adopted handheld computing at an accelerated rate. One recent survey reports 64 percent of respondents reported using PDAs in clinical practice (MediClicks, 2003). The PDA is becoming an indispensable tool, or as it's being called by some, "the new black bag" (Shipman, 2001, 224). Handheld computing is considered a valuable tool in various fields of medicine and reports of its use are reflected in that literature (Fischler, 2003). Several factors have spurred this rapid growth including mobility, affordability, size, ease of use, and the breadth of available medical applications (Shaw, 2001). Physicians and other hospital personnel are turning to these devices for reference information, clinical decision-making, patient tracking, and prescription writing. Used as an interactive device at the bedside, the latest protocol or lab results are just a tap away. Academic health centers are exploring ways that PDA technology can be integrated into medical education as a teaching aid, an evaluation tool, and as a log to record experiences, procedures, and patient interactions for students and residents. Students find them invaluable as a stand-alone resource at the bedside for information on drugs, diagnosis and practice guidelines. An increasing number of health sciences education programs are requiring students to purchase PDAs along with the standard list of required textbooks. For all of these reasons, health sciences libraries are making the decision to support and promote PDAs as a natural extension of their services. This paper provides an overview of the approaches being used to incorporate PDAs into academic health center and hospital libraries and highlights the role of the reference librarian.

## ADOPTION AND IMMERSION

Health sciences libraries are responding to users' needs, and are in many cases leading their institutions, in the integration and support of PDAs (Stoddard, 2001). Libraries that embrace PDAs elect to support the technology to varying degrees. PDA services might include provision of hardware, software, resource information, Web pages, consultation, training and technical support. The selection of PDA services is driven in large part by available resources, infrastructure and administrative support. Development of a PDA support policy will further define the library's role for users and ensure that efforts are scalable and sustainable.

However, even with a PDA support policy, barriers may prevent or impede implementation of PDA services. Zaroukian (2002) reviews the barriers of handheld computing in a medical residency program and cites time, financial cost, and inadequate institutional support as the greatest impediments. Health sciences libraries face many of the same barriers. Supporting a new technology, and with it, another publication format, is expensive not only in terms of budget, but in staff time and training as well. Group licensing agreements for products are costly and may be viewed as an unnecessary duplication and expense if the resource is already available in another format. PDA users need access to a computer for synchronization, and access to the Internet for interactive products that provide regular updates. Libraries that elect to incorporate synchronization into PDA services need open access to their computers. Frequently, however, hospital and academic Instructional Technology (IT) departments restrict read/write access making this kind of service difficult.

Crowell and Shaw-Kokot (2003) lay out a four-step approach that begins with getting library staff involved with PDAs before they assist other departments in integrating these tools in the instructional program. Smith (2003) echoes the strategy of getting librarians involved first before teaching others and adds the objective of developing or providing PDA-deliverable content. When family practice residents at Middlesex Hospital in Connecticut were given Palm IIIx devices, the librarian recruited one of the residents, known as the "Palm Wizard," to orient her to the devices. Once she had a solid PDA foundation she purchased cradles for the library and was able to provide technical support (Morgen, 2003, 13).

## SELECTION OF SERVICES

### Supporting the Container

Technical support continues to be the hot potato of PDAs. When use of handhelds began to take off in the late 1990s, hospital and academic

IT departments were reluctant to take on responsibility for yet another operating system. The immersion in the new technology competed with large wireless and network update projects. Security issues relating to the Health Information Portability and Accountability Act (HIPAA) that went into effect in April 2003 were additional stumbling blocks. Handheld users turned to the library for support.

Providing patrons with devices to sample was a feature of several early PDA projects. Offering users a chance to try before they buy proved to be an effective way to introduce new users to the possibilities of the technology. At Texas A&M University's Medical Science Library, librarian Joe Williams was responsible for developing new library services in a wireless environment. The library purchased two Visor Pro PDAs to be circulated to patrons as a way to promote the technology (Williams, 2003). Some libraries also included pre-loaded applications on devices loaned for trial. In 2000, the University of Illinois at Chicago, Library of the Health Sciences-Peoria (LHS-Peoria) was asked to set up, distribute and support fifty Handspring Visor Deluxe devices, each pre-loaded with several freeware medical applications, to third-year medical students. In addition, the library provided PDA compatible copies of the *Washington Manual of Therapeutics*, *Harrison's Companion Handbook*, *5 Minute Clinical Consult* and *Lexi Drugs* for students to trial during their Internal Medicine rotation. During a joint project, funded by the Illinois State Library, the Library Resource Center of OSF St. Francis Medical Center (OSF Library), and the LHS-Peoria made available a total of thirty-five handheld devices, each pre-loaded with subject-specific content, for users to trial. The final grant report is available at http://library.osfsaintfrancis.org/pdagrant. htm.[1] [Note: Web sites are also listed in the order that they appear here in an appendix at the end of the article–the editors.] This project included circulation of peripheral devices including keyboards, cameras, voice recorders, and Margi Presenter-To-Go, a presentation device that facilitates PowerPoint presentations from a handheld, http://www.margi. com/.[2] In today's rapidly evolving handheld market, however, providing hardware for users to trial is becoming cost-prohibitive.

In addition to circulating handhelds for trial, libraries have also provided device-specific synchronization cradles. As early as 1993, the Health Sciences Library at the University of Arizona (AHSL) provided cradles in the library for HP95LX palmtops that had been distributed to medical and nursing students. By 1998, they added synchronization (sync) hardware for Palm III, Palm V and Handspring Visors (Stoddard, 2001). As the flavors of devices have increased so has the challenge to provide sync stations for those devices. Libraries are turning to infrared sync stations that can accommodate a variety of handheld devices. The University of Alberta has a pilot program, the PDA Infrared Beaming Station, http://www.library.ualberta.ca/pdazone/beaming/index.cfm,[3] that enables students to beam results from a database or catalog search to the handheld. At Yale's Harvey Cushing/John Hay Whitney Medical Library, a wireless EthIR port provides students infrared sync access, http://www.med.yale.edu/library/projects/infrared/.[4] Access is to AvantGo, http://www.avantgo.com,[5] a Web browsing application and ePocrates, http://www.epocrates.com,[6] a widely used drug compendium.

An important issue regarding public sync stations is, of course, privacy. Password-protected access to sync capability may be one solution. Beyond that, users can be encouraged to take advantage of the password protection built into devices, or subscribe to third-party security applications. Restricting access to select conduits is another option for libraries that want to provide synchronization to specific programs, such as ePocrates or AvantGo.

Medical reference librarians today must be prepared to answer a myriad of technical questions about computers, other hardware in general, and PDAs specifically. It is important for medical libraries to provide staff with devices in order for them to become familiar with the many issues related to handheld use. This is a must if the library is committed to providing technical support for these devices. This service may be an adjunct to what the IT department provides, or, in some cases, may be the only resource for users.

## Supporting the Content

Current PDA projects tend to focus more on the content than the container. As recently as five years ago, only a small number of well-regarded medical applications were available for the handheld. The demands on the medical librarian for help in identifying, locating and acquiring applications were manageable. With the ever-growing number of medical applications, selecting the best or most suitable has become a daunting task. Hattery states, "The IT department may support and give guidance on the hardware and operating system. But it is up to the librarian to advise on content" (2001). Whether individual, group, or site licenses are the goal, libraries must increasingly contend with procurement limitations and access control.

## Stand-Alone Reference Resources

Some early PDA projects offered trial software to users, but increasingly, publishers of medical applications offer a trial or demo version. Stand-alone applications transformed the physician's PDA from a personal information device to a portable medical reference library with applications such as *Taber's Cyclopedic Medical Dictionary* or the *Physician's Desk Reference*. Libraries are now looking to institutional licensing to make applications available to their users. Some libraries such as the Learning Resource Center, University of Arkansas for Medical Sciences (UAMS Library), http://www.library.uams.edu/lrc/pdainfo/pdalibrary.htm,[7] have also negotiated agreements with PDA content developers such as Skyscape, http://www.skyscape.com,[8] and Handheldmed, http://www.handheldmed.com,[9] for discounts on their products.

## Databases

Ovid@Hand, http://www.ovid@hand.com,[10] powered by Unbound Medicine, http://www.unboundmedicine.com,[11] was an early contender for PDA database integration. Ovid@Hand provides a PDA interface for Ovid MEDLINE in addition to a drug information database and table of contents from a user-selected list of medical journals. Users that participated in the OSF Library/LHS-Peoria project were among the first to try Ovid@Hand. The University of Virginia Health Sciences Library (UVa-HSL) provides site-licensed applications to mobileMICROMEDEX, http://www.micromedex.com/products/mobilemicromedex/,[12] a comprehensive drug database, and InfoPOEMS, http://www.infopoems.com/,[13] a clinical awareness information system. Affiliates of the UAMS Library can take advantage of discounts on applications such as Clinical Pharmacology On Hand and MICROMEDEX. Libraries that already subscribe to MDConsult, http://www.mdconsult.com,[14] now have MDCMobile, MDConsult's handheld interface, as an additional database offering for their PDA users. MDCMobile content includes daily news updates, drug alerts, user-selected journal abstracts, and a search interface for the PDA. The National Library of Medicine (NLM) has a free Web application designed to search PubMed, http://archive.nlm.nih.gov/proj/pmot/eval.php,[15] read journal abstracts, and access ClinicalTrials.gov, http://www.clinicaltrials.gov,[16] using wireless, handheld computers.

## *Original Content*

In addition to commercial fare, libraries are implementing unique PDA resources and developing custom content. The University of Georgia Libraries have created a "Handheld Users Guide to your PDA," http://www.libs.uga.edu/pda/#,[17] an interactive assistant that allows users to browse call numbers or ask a reference question. Yale Medical Library, http://www.med.yale.edu/library/pdachannel/,[18] The University of North Carolina Health Sciences Library (UNC-HSL), http://www.hsl.unc.edu/pda/hslpda.cfm,[19] and Denison Memorial Library at the University of Colorado Health Sciences Center (UCHSC), are only a few of the libraries that have developed PDA friendly guides to library services and resources. Most of these resources are accessible through AvantGo, a free Web browser, as a custom channel.

## *PROMOTION*

Medical libraries are actively promoting the use of PDAs to their constituents through special events, Web sites, user groups and instruction. The Duke University Medical Center Library (DUMCL) "Using PDAs" tutorial, http://www.mclibrary.duke.edu/respub/guides/pdatutorial/,[20] includes a terminology section, a list of "How-to" links, and tips and tricks. Dartmouth Biomedical Libraries presented "The Handheld PDA: a valuable clinical information tool," http://www.dartmouth.edu/~biomed/new.htmld/lgr_pda.shtml,[21] as part of their regular Library Grand Rounds series. The session included an overview of the technology and updates on PDA initiatives at Dartmouth. DUMCL and UNC-HSL partnered to present Mobile Forums, monthly meetings that include an hour program followed by an hour discussion (Moore, 2002).

PDA user groups have proven to be an effective way to promote PDA activity and share practical information about their use. At the Brittingham Memorial Library, MetroHealth Medical Center (Cleveland), Steve Grove, and Christine Dziedzina joined with area physicians to form the PDA Library Users Group (PLUG) (Dziedzina, 2003). The group developed a PDA use policy and recommended " OnlyMe" as the security software for all hospital handheld devices.

Special events are another effective way to introduce the technology and library services. DUMCL and UNC-HSL co-sponsored a Mobile Technology Fair in 2002 with grant funds from the National Library of Medicine. Events included presentations, demonstrations and vendor exhibits. One of the components of the joint OSF Library/LHS-Peoria LSTA grant was hosting an all day PDA seminar that included a four-hour continuing education course and panel discussions. University of Southern California's Norris Medical Library sponsored PDA fairs in 2001 and 2002 that included vendor exhibits and demonstration sessions and offered PDA products as raffle prizes.

### PDA Web Site

Perhaps the one universal feature of library PDA initiatives is a PDA Web site. Common elements of medical library PDA sites include PDA basics and links to hardware and software resources. More ambitious sites include extensive resource links and institution-specific information. As decision-making continues to be an obstacle for users, some sites offer recommendations for software, or provide links to independent reviews of programs. Linking to major PDA portals that publish reviews of applications beyond the publisher's own descriptions can be invaluable to users and librarians. Some academic libraries have identified a list of "core content" or a "select list" for specific patron populations. The LHS-Peoria has a "Select List of PDA Applications" that includes links to basic information about the product, vendors and independent reviews, http://www.uic.edu/depts/lib/lhsp/temp/pdaselect.htm.[22] Subject-specific Web pages are another way that libraries provide detailed information about applications available in a particular discipline such as Pediatrics or Psychiatry.

The University of Maryland's Health Sciences and Human Services Library has developed "Personalized Digital Assistants–Going Mobile," http://www.hshsl.umaryland.edu/resources/pdainfo/res.html,[23] that provides the latest information on hardware, evaluation resources, user resources, and a PDA user list. The Lyman Maynard Stowe Library of the University of Connecticut Health Center's PDA Resources, http://library.uchc.edu/pda/,[24] includes extensive resource pages with information on PDA databases, a section on security issues, PDA news and operating system-specific resources. The AHSL offers a blend of medical and general PDA resources as well as PDA library services geared to their own patrons. A PDA bibliography with 659 citations can also be found at http://educ.ahsl.arizona.edu/pda/index.htm.[25] UVa-HSL offers help for the PDA novice by providing guides to buying a device, viewing various material formats on a PDA, and security information. Megan Fox, Simmons College Libraries, provides an extensive listing of PDA projects and initiatives at other libraries and universities, a com-

prehensive resource not found elsewhere, http://web.simmons.edu/
~fox/PDA.html#list_type.[26]

## *INSTRUCTION*

PDAs present numerous instructional opportunities and challenges
for reference librarians as instruction may take many forms. Traditional
classes and seminars are good starting points for promoting the use of
PDAs and introducing the basics of standard functions and synchronization. In 1997, when the AHSL implemented support for the Palm OS,
training consisted of campus announcements for free consultation sessions (Stoddard, 2001). Early teaching sessions were facilitated using
an Elmo or a freely available Palm emulator program. More recently
Margi Presenter-To-Go's Margi Mirror component has become a convenient way to show new users around the Palm device. Classes designed for targeted audiences with special subject interests can be a
successful approach. During the OSF Library/LHS-Peoria PDA project, instructors developed sessions that presented resources specific to
clinicians in select disciplines. Targeted groups included hospital phar-
macists, pediatric residents and attendings, and surgery residents and
attendings.

As a result of an overwhelming response to a "Medical Informatics
Seminar," USC Norris Medical Library purchased Palm VIIx handhelds for librarians with the stipulation that they sync to the library's
calendar system. "The library's goal is to facilitate the integration of
handheld technology into the culture of the university's health sciences
campus" (Smith, 2002, 94). At the University of Buffalo, "Getting to
Know Your PDA" sessions are regularly offered (Fox, 2003). Libraries
like the AHSL and the University of Washington Health Sciences Libraries (UWHSL) have offered regular workshops for faculty and students. At UWHSL, "Palm Pilot Solutions for the Busy Academician"
was co-presented by a librarian and a clinician. The availability of
PubMed on Tap, the PDA version of PubMed (MEDLINE) from NLM,
along with other medical databases in PDA format, creates an expanded
role for librarians that extends beyond technology training to information management education.

### *Consultation*

The personal nature of handheld computing creates unique needs for
each user. One-on-one consultations are often the most satisfactory way

to acclimate a new user. Among the most frequently sought advice is information and direction about what kind of device to purchase. Whether to purchase a Palm OS device or a device running Pocket PC or Windows CE operating systems impact on applications available. Some hospitals and universities recommend one or two specific handheld brands or devices. When this is not the case, a buying guide or links to other buying guides can be most beneficial to users. Another stumbling block for new PDA users is getting software from the vendor to the device. For novice users the download and installation process can be perplexing. Some applications, such as ePocrates, are even more complex because there are two applications that work together. Frequently students need help getting this resource to load successfully.

Individualized instruction may be the most appropriate for PDAs because of the customizability, availability of multiple models, and different operating platforms. In addition, users have a variety of instructional needs dependent upon their level of comfort with the technology, intended use, and available content. Although this is a time-intensive alternative, it is probably the most successful. Challenges abound for reference librarians from unannounced requests for instruction, the need for familiarity with a multitude of handheld models, and the plethora of applications. A possible solution is the establishment of PDA office hours or an appointment only policy. Another protection for library staff time is a well-defined support policy that delineates which platforms and applications the library supports.

### PDAs in the Curriculum

Curricular needs are driving the incorporation of PDAs for use by nursing and medical students as well as in postgraduate medical education in academic health centers and teaching hospitals. Numerous reports in the medical and nursing literature describe ways in which PDAs are being used. Huffstutler (2002) reports integrating handheld technology into the nursing curriculum in order to role model the use of the technology. Students were required to use a PDA for the pharmacology course instead of a textbook, and were referred to PDA programs for preparation of case studies. Speedie et al. (2002) outline ways to use PDAs to support medical students in outpatient clinical clerkships to provide: readily available reference materials at the practice sites; a means for students to collect required patient encounter information at the point of care; and a method to record and submit evaluations of teaching. Medical residents have found a variety of ways to use handhelds, including downloading information, using spreadsheets for common formulas, and searching MEDLINE with modem or wireless access (Beasley, 2002). In particular, the evidence-based medicine (EBM) curriculum, which focuses on the use of the medical literature for clinical decision-making and life-long learning, encourages the use of PDAs as an information tool at the point of care. At the LHS-Peoria, an EBM course for third-year medical students was the impetus for the incorporation of PDAs into library services. The pilot project, funded by the Illinois Alliance Library System, provided PDA-delivered content for use by students during their Internal Medicine clerkship, the point in the curriculum in which they learn EBM and critical appraisal skills. Project evaluation suggested that accessibility at the point of care increased students' use of the resources and resulted in better patient care decisions (Dorsch, 2001). DUMCL developed a PDA friendly EBM Toolkit, http://www.mclibrary.duke.edu/respub/pdaformat/ebm.html,[27] that includes a section on terminology, a MEDLINE tutorial, and a quick reference section. The toolkit can be downloaded to a handheld via AvantGo.

## WHAT NEXT?

Mobile technologies are providing new opportunities for library services. The widespread adoption of handheld computing by the medical profession provides health sciences librarians exciting opportunities for new services and opens the door for innovative and collaborative projects with other departments within the hospital or academic institution or with other libraries.

### Wireless Access to Resources

Wireless access to the library's online catalog, databases, and full-text journals will soon be standard library fare. The day is approaching when reference librarians will cruise the library, PDA in hand, and offer assistance to patrons in the stacks or in reading rooms. In response to a question, the librarian will wirelessly access the online catalog or an appropriate database and within moments have an answer in the palm of the hand. Librarians will be able to beam patron-specific information such as due dates or search results, directly to the handheld. Patrons can look forward to accessing library resources anytime, anywhere. Several products are already well established as library-friendly.

Clarinet, http://www.clarinetsys.com,[28] provides network access for PDAs, cell phones, and other Ethernet-enabled devices. Himmelford Health Sciences Library at the George Washington University Medical Center provides synchronization to AvantGo and Epocrates using a Clarinet infrared device that supports both Palm OS and Pocket PC. TriBeam Technologies offers Extended Range Infrared Communications (ERIC), http://www.tribeam.com/,[29] that takes advantage of the native infrared capabilities in PDAs to facilitate two-way communication with beam stations. Installing the ERIC software enables the handheld device to access the Web wirelessly.

## *CONCLUSION*

Reflecting on the role of medical libraries, Lucretia McClure reminds us, "from the perspective of 35 years . . . our basic job is still the same. We still want to give people the best source, the best information, in the best way we can" (Quoted in Clemmons, 2001). How that source is identified, how the best information is ferreted, and how we present it to the patron, are things that have changed drastically with technology. While the information is much more accessible to the end user, it is still the job of the reference librarian to understand how that information is organized, how best to retrieve and filter it, and how best to manage it once it has been harvested.

Beyond its value as a freestanding reference tool, PDAs are increasingly being used as an interactive device. Physicians depend on the latest news, drug alerts, and journal contents to keep up in every day practice. The wireless environment adds another dimension by bringing MEDLINE search results to the bedside. More than ever health professionals will need core information competencies in literature searching, critical appraisal, and bibliographic management. Bibliographic instruction and information literacy remain priorities, but how these services are facilitated is changing. Strategies for serving distant patrons will drive library resources and services, digital content, and infrastructure decision-making. Medical librarians must remain proactive in their approach to technology. In the short term, medical libraries can offer wireless access to the online catalog, bibliographic databases, and full-text journals. In the long term we can work to provide digital content that will reside on a personal device for a finite or indefinite period of time as we develop strategies that will help our patrons manage the avalanche of options for both content and container.

Librarians led the way in the adoption of the personal computer as an information tool and expanded their teaching roles as end-user database searching became ubiquitous. Once again we're challenged to meet the information needs of users by providing services, instruction, and content for a new technology. Using a variety of approaches, medical libraries have quickly adopted this technology to deliver medical information in a non-traditional way. Peters et al. (2003) suggest, "In some ways the PDA movement is similar to what happened with the web. Both threaten to overwhelm libraries, librarianship, and information science." Librarians must develop strategies for keeping pace with this rapidly evolving market and translate those developments into new programs and services. "PDAs represent the potential congruence of all types of information onto a single device, as well as the congruence of synchronous and asynchronous communication . . . " (Peters et al., 2003). It can also be said that library PDA initiatives epitomize the congruence of information services, patron population, and newly emerging technologies.

## REFERENCES

21st Century Medicine: technology and physicians: recent survey results, 2003. *MediClicks* 1, 43 (March). Available online, http://www.mediclicks.net/issues/article43_1.asp.

Beasley, Brent W, 2002. Utility of palmtop computers in a residency program: a pilot study. *Southern Medical Journal* 95, no. 2 (February):207-211.

Clemmons, Nancy W, 2001. Lucretia's view: an interview with Lucretia W. McClure about medical reference through the years, February 25, 2000. *Medical Reference Services Quarterly* 20, no. 1 (Spring):1-10.

Crowell, Karen and Julia Shaw-Kokot., 2003. Extending the hand of knowledge: promoting mobile technologies. *Medical Reference Services Quarterly* 22, no. 1 (Spring):1-9.

Dorsch, Jo, 2001. PDA Information Technology at the Bedside. "Light My Fire" Final Report. http://www.uic.edu/depts/lib/lhsp/temp/lmf1.pdf.

Dziedzina, Christine, 2003. PDAs at MHMC: The Brittingham Memorial Library PDA Program. *E-Sources*, no. 7 (Jan-March).

Fischler, Sandra, Thomas E. Stewart, Sangeeta Meiita, Randy Wax, and Stephen E. Lapinsky, 2003. Handheld computing in medicine. *Journal of the American Medical Informatics Association* 10, no. 2 (March/April): 139-149.

Fox, Megan K., 2003. "A library in your palm." *NetConnect* (Spring): 10-15.

Hattery, M., 2001. The PDA: its place in the library. *Information Retrieval and Library Automation* 36 (12).

Huffstutler, Shelly, Tami H. Wyatt, and Cherie P. Wright, 2002. The use of handheld technology in nursing education. *Nurse Educator* 26, no. 6 (November/December): 271-275.

Moore, Margaret E. and Julia Shaw Kokot, 2002. Mobile technology forums. *Medical Reference Services Quarterly*, 21, no. 2 (Summer): 75-79.

Morgen, Evelyn Breck, 2003. Implementing PDA technology in a medical library: experiences in a hospital library and an academic medical center library. *Medical Reference Services Quarterly*, 22, no. 1 (Spring): 11-19.

Peters, Tom, Josephine Dorsch, Lori Bell, and Peg Burnette, 2003. "PDAs and Health Science Libraries," *Library Hi Tech* 21, no. 4.

Shah, Maulin, 2001. Grassroots computing: palmtops in health care. *Journal of the American Medical Association* 285, no. 13 (4 April): 1768.

Shipman, Jean P. and Andrew C. Morton, 2001. The new black bag: PDAs, health care and library services. *Reference Services Review* 29, no. 3: 229.

Smith, Russell, 2003. Adopting a new technology to the academic medical library: personal digital assistants. *Journal of the Medical Library Association* 90, no. 1 (January): 93-94.

Speedie, Stuart, James Pacala, Gregory Vercellotti, Ilene Harris, and Xinyu Zhou, 2002. PDA support for outpatient clinical clerkships: mobile computing for medical education. *Proceedings of the American Medical Informatics Association Annual Symposium*: 207-211.

Stoddard, Mari J., 2001. Handhelds in the health sciences library. *Medical Reference Services Quarterly* 20, no. 3 (Fall): 75-82.

Williams, Joe, 2003. Taming the wireless frontier: PDAs, tablets and laptops at home on the range. *Computers in Libraries* 23, no. 3 (March): 10-12, 62-4.

Zaroukian, Michael H., 2002. Handheld computing in resident education: benefits, barriers, and considerations. *Seminars in Medical Practice* 5, no. 4 (December): 33-44.

APPENDIX. Web Sites

1. Library Resource Center, OSF St. Francis Medical Center, PDA Grant, http://library.osfsaintfrancis.org/pdagrant.htm
2. Margi Presenter-to-Go, http://www.margi.com/
3. University of Alberta Libraries, PDA Infrared (IR) Beaming Station, http://www.library.ualberta.ca/pdazone/beaming/index.cfm
4. Yale University, Harvey Cushing/John Hay Whitney Medical Library, Synchronize your PDA with the Wireless EthIR Lan Port in the Medical Library, http://www.med.yale.edu/library/projects/infrared/
5. AvantGo, http://www.avantgo.com
6. Epocrates, http://www.epocrates.com
7. University of Arkansas Medical Sciences, Learning Resource Center, PDA Information, http://www.library.uams.edu/lrc/pdainfo/pdalibrary.htm
8. SkyScape, http://www.skyscape.com
9. HandHeldMed, http://www.handheldmed.com
10. Ovid@Hand, http://www.ovid@hand.com
11. Unbound Medicine, http://www.unboundmedicine.com
12. MICROMEDEX, http://www.micromedex.com/products/mobilemicromedex/
13. InfoPOEMs, http://www.infopoems.com
14. MDConsult, http://www.mdconsult.com
15. PubMed On Tap (an application for PDAs), http://archive.nlm.nih.gov/proj/pmot/eval.php
16. ClinicalTrials.gov, National Institutes of Health, http://www.clinicaltrials.gov
17. University of Georgia Libraries, Handheld Users Guide, http://www.libs.uga.edu/pda/#
18. Yale University, Harvey Cushing/John Hay Whitney Medical Library, PDA Channel Home Page, http://www.med.yale.edu/library/pdachannel/
19. University of North Carolina-Chapel Hill, Health Sciences Library, Accessing HSL information on your PDA!, http://www.hsl.unc.edu/pda/hslpda.cfm
20. Duke University, Medical Center Library, Tutorials: Using Personal Digital Assistants (PDAs), http://www.mclibrary.duke.edu/respub/guides/pdatutorial/
21. Dartmouth Biomedical Libraries, The Handheld PDA, http://www.dartmouth.edu/~biomed/new.htmld/lgr_pda.shtml

APPENDIX (continued)

22. University of Illinois Chicago, Library of the Health Sciences-Peoria, Select List of PDA Applications,
    http://www.uic.edu/depts/lib/lhsp/temp/pdaselect.htm
23. University of Maryland, Health Sciences & Human Services Library, Personal Digital Assistants-Going Mobile,
    http://www.hshsl.umaryland.edu/resources/pdainfo/res.html
24. University of Connecticut Health Center, Lyman Maynard Stowe Library, PDA Resource, http://library.uchc.edu/pda/
25. Arizona Health Sciences Library, PDAs for Health Care Providers, http://educ.ahsl.arizona.edu/pda/index.htm
26. Simmons College Libraries, PDAs and Handhelds in Libraries and Academia, http://web.simmons.edu/~fox/PDA.html#list_type
27. Duke University, Medical Center Library, EBM Tool Kit,
    http://www.mclibrary.duke.edu/respub/pdaformat/ebm.html
28. Clarient Systems, Wireless Connectivity for Handheld Devices,
    http://www.clarinetsys.com
29. TriBeam, Wireless Internet Access, http://www.tribeam.com

# E-Mail Reference Evaluation:
# Using the Results of a Satisfaction Survey

Leanne M. VandeCreek

**SUMMARY.** E-mail reference has been utilized as a reference tool in academic libraries since the early 1980s. Today it is one of the most common media for providing digital reference service. An important aspect of providing any service is evaluating users' satisfaction levels with that service. Users of the Ask-A-Librarian e-mail reference service at a large academic library over a ten-month period voluntarily completed a seven item web-based questionnaire. The results indicated that the majority of respondents were satisfied with Ask-A-Librarian overall. This paper discusses how the library used the survey results to improve the existing service, and to implement a new one-chat reference. Reference service providers should not only ask users for feedback on existing services, but also should include them in the planning and design phase of new services. In doing so, they demonstrate their commitment to providing adequate and appropriate services to their patron community, and ultimately can save their institutions time and expense. *[Article copies available for a fee from The Haworth Document Delivery Service: 1-800-HAWORTH. E-mail address: <docdelivery@haworthpress.com> Website: <http://www.HaworthPress.com> © 2006 by The Haworth Press, Inc. All rights reserved.]*

Leanne M. VandeCreek is Social Science Reference Librarian and Assistant Professor, Northern Illinois University Libraries, DeKalb, IL 60115 (E-mail: lvandecreek@niu.edu).

[Haworth co-indexing entry note]: "E-Mail Reference Evaluation: Using the Results of a Satisfaction Survey." VandeCreek, Leanne M. Co-published simultaneously in *The Reference Librarian* (The Haworth Information Press, an imprint of The Haworth Press, Inc.) No. 93, 2006, pp. 99-108; and: *New Directions in Reference* (ed: Byron Anderson, and Paul T. Webb) The Haworth Information Press, an imprint of The Haworth Press, Inc., 2006, pp. 99-108. Single or multiple copies of this article are available for a fee from The Haworth Document Delivery Service [1-800-HAWORTH, 9:00 a.m. - 5:00 p.m. (EST). E-mail address: docdelivery@haworthpress.com].

doi:10.1300/J120v45n93_08

**KEYWORDS.** Academic libraries, Ask-A-Librarian e-mail reference, chat reference, digital reference service, evaluation, surveys, user feedback, user satisfaction, user involvement, user consultation

E-mail reference is not a new concept in academic librarianship. Academic libraries first began experimenting with e-mail as a reference medium in the early 1980s (Gross, McClure, & Lankes, 2003). By the mid-1990s, many college and university libraries successfully used e-mail as a major reference tool. Today, the number of academic libraries providing e-mail reference continues to grow, making e-mail "the most common vehicle for providing digital references service" (Gross et al., 2003), though for the most part it is just one of many tools used to provide digital reference services.

Much of the library literature on e-mail based reference services focuses on issues surrounding the design and implementation of such services: what to expect, do's and don'ts, policy, and procedure (Weissman, 2001; Tomaiuolo & Packer, 2000; Gray, 2000; Lankes & Kasowitz, 1998; Staley, 1998; Powell & Bradigan, 2001). Journal articles frequently report campus-specific e-mail reference experiences in the form of case studies, commonly offering descriptive data such as the number and types of questions asked (Bushallow-Wilber, Devinney, & Whitcomb, 1996; Frank, 1998; Diamond & Pease, 2001; Lederer, 2001).

As the repertoire of public services in the digital environment grows, librarians have begun to recognize the need for, and importance of, evaluating and/or assessing patrons' satisfaction level with e-mail reference services. As Horn and Kjaer (2000) state, "the main purpose of an evaluation of an electronic reference service is to assure that the goals and objectives of the service are being met and to ascertain that the service is working efficiently and effectively" (p. 138). The monthly question totals and categorization frequently offered in the literature and in typical internal reporting structures tell us only that the service is being used, and for what purposes. Those statistics alone, however, neither reveal whether patrons' information needs are being adequately met, whether the service might need revamping or improving, nor how to go about implementing any desired changes. This article discusses an analysis of user satisfaction with the e-mail based Ask-A-Librarian service at Northern Illinois University (NIU), and how the results of the analysis were utilized by administration and reference staff.

In the spring of 2002, the NIU Libraries received funding though the NIU Office of the Provost to perform user satisfaction studies on a variety of library services. Ask-A-Librarian was one of the public services selected for analysis. There were increasing numbers of patrons using the service each month. However, little was known about patrons' satisfaction level, except for anecdotal evidence, as no means to systematically measure satisfaction level was in place. User surveys provide the opportunity to gain a measure of satisfaction based on user perception. While evaluating the quality of reference responses to users' questions is another very important component of electronic reference service, it was not explored in this initial study.

## *METHODOLOGY*

The University Libraries hired NIU's Social Science Research Institute (SSRI) to assist in the design and implementation of the analysis project. Library administrators, faculty and staff involved in the Ask-A-Librarian service met with a representative of SSRI and formed an Advisory Group to discuss the goals of the project.

The group first discussed how best to solicit feedback from Ask-A-Librarian users. It became clear that electronic surveys were the best option. Some advantages to electronic surveys are: efficiency, as responses can be received quickly; cost effectiveness, because no copying or postage fees are incurred; and increased accuracy in recording responses. Data entry errors can be eliminated by automatically building responses into a database (Lazar & Preece, 2001). Lazar and Preece also describe two major possible disadvantages to electronic survey methods as well: difficulty in identifying survey respondents and difficulty in ensuring a representative sample. In this case, the survey population was well-defined–all Ask-A-Librarian patrons who had used the service from the time that tracking questions and answers was started until the time of the survey.

As with any survey, the Advisory Group was faced with the possibility that respondents would not necessarily be representative of the entire population, and therefore care was taken not to make broad generalizations based on the survey results. With this in mind, the Advisory Group decided that an online survey, with the embedded link e-mailed to everyone who had used the service, would be the most effective method for collecting the data.

The next step was designing the survey. As with paper surveys, electronic surveys must have clear and unambiguous wording so the recipients are not confused about what is being asked (Lazar and Preece, 1999). The Advisory Group constructed a seven-item questionnaire based on the information they desired from the participants. After pre-testing the survey questions with the ten most recent users of Ask-A-Librarian, it was clear that the wording of three of the questions was misleading. The questions were rewritten, and again distributed to the ten most recent users of Ask-A-Librarian. This time the respondents demonstrated a clear understanding of what was being asked, and all members of the Advisory Group approved the final version of the questionnaire (see Appendix).

Six of the seven questions were closed-ended (multiple choice), soliciting information about use of the service, satisfaction with the answer(s) received and response time, and an overall rating of the service. The seventh item was open-ended, encouraging the patron to offer positive or negative feedback, or any suggestions they might have for improving the service.

Patrons submitted their Ask-A-Librarian queries via an online Web form linked from the library's Web site. The form asked for the following information: name, telephone number, e-mail address, status (faculty, staff, undergraduate, graduate, other), campus (DeKalb campus, branch campus, or satellite location), and their question. None of the fields were mandatory. Obviously, if the patron provided no, or inaccurate, telephone and e-mail address information, there was no way to respond to the query.

The e-mail addresses only (and no other personal identifying information) of patrons utilizing Ask-A-Librarian from March 2001 through January 2002 (a total of 499 people) were provided to the SSRI. The SSRI sent a message with an embedded link to the Web-based survey to each address. The message also advised users that participation in the survey was voluntary. Repeat users of the service (as indicated by their e-mail address appearing more than once in the list) were sent only one message.

## RESULTS

After two requests for participation, a total of 167 completed surveys were received. Of the 499 e-mails sent, 48 were returned as "undeliverable." The overall response rate was 33 percent; removal of the "undeliverable" messages resulted in a response rate of 37 percent.

Results indicated that the principal users of Ask-A-Librarian were graduate students (44 percent), followed by undergraduates (25 percent), and faculty members (21 percent). The top two reasons given for using the Ask-A-Librarian service were: assistance with a graduate research paper and technical help using library resources. (See Table 1.) The main reasons noted by respondents under "Other" were assistance with interlibrary loan, book renewal, and navigating the library's new Web site.

The majority of respondents, 91 percent, indicated they got the information they needed, and 75 percent indicated the response they received was "Very Helpful." Ninety-two percent rated the Ask-A-Librarian service as either "Excellent" or "Good." Ninety-three percent of respondents rated the service as being "Very Prompt" or "Prompt." Nearly two-thirds (65 percent) responded that having a response to their question within 48 hours was adequate, while 34 percent indicated they needed a faster response time.

## DISCUSSION

The results of the survey were useful to the library in several ways. Patron feedback provided convincing evidence of users' satisfaction with the existing Ask-A-Librarian service. The statistics indicate that the majority of survey respondents (92 percent) were satisfied overall with the Ask-A-Librarian service. Survey results also revealed some of the strengths and shortcomings of other library services as well. The

TABLE 1. Reasons for Using Ask-A-Librarian

| Reason | Percent* | Number |
|---|---|---|
| Graduate research paper | 31% | 52 |
| For technical help in using library resources | 30% | 50 |
| Help in getting into a database | 21% | 35 |
| Undergraduate term paper | 16% | 26 |
| Faculty research | 10% | 17 |
| Other | 20% | 33 |

*Since respondents could check as many as apply, the percentages total more than 100 percent.

most common response in this regard was a request to have interlibrary loan arrival notifications be delivered via e-mail, not regular mail. The NIU Libraries has modified and improved its existing services and has even implemented new services based on these unexpected but helpful results.

In three instances, patrons indicated they did not remember utilizing the Ask-A-Librarian service, perhaps due to the passage of time between using the service and receiving the survey. Future surveys may have a higher response rate if the survey is administered to the patrons immediately or shortly after the service is first used.

Perhaps the most valuable survey results were the responses to the open-ended questions 1 and 7. For Question 1, "What is the main reason why you used 'Ask-A-Librarian'? Check all that apply," many respondents selected "Other (specify)" as their answer. Their comments illuminate the variety of users other than NIU faculty, staff and students accessing the service, for example, alumni, general public, high school students and professionals, and their diverse information needs, for example, professional research, job support, and locating obscure items. Such variety seems to indicate that any Ask-A-Librarian service is likely viewed not as merely a means for online ready reference service, but more broadly, as a way for all patrons to contact and communicate with the library, no matter what their needs might be.

Question 7 afforded patrons the opportunity to suggest ways in which the NIU Libraries might improve its Ask-A-Librarian service. Thirty-three respondents simply offered kudos on a job well done, or indicated they could not think of any specific things to be done to make it better. However, ten patrons did offer suggestions to improve the service.

One patron stated, "Make sure that people know about this great service." At the time, there was only one link to the Ask-A-Librarian Web form on the library's homepage, but when the library site was redesigned, a link to Ask-A-Librarian was placed on every page. It is difficult to predict when a patron's question may arise, so it is good design to have the link prominently displayed in numerous places on the site.

Another patron wrote, "The ability to talk or e-mail directly to your faculty at the library would be helpful. There is no substitute for good personal contact. . . . " At the time of the survey, contact information (phone number, e-mail address, office number) for library personnel was available on the library's Web site, but somewhat difficult to find. When the site was redesigned, and in addition to the "Personnel and Departments" listings, subject specialist librarians' contact information was placed at the top of each "Databases by Subject" page for convenience (see http://www.niulib.niu.edu/psychology.cfm for an example of such a page on the NIU Libraries Web site). For example, the Psychology Librarian's contact information is on the Psychology subject page, the English Librarian's information is on the English page, etc.

As mentioned earlier, approximately 65 percent of respondents indicated that receiving a response to their question within 48 hours was satisfactory. While this pleased the Ask-A-Librarian Coordinator and Library Administration, the remaining 34 percent (or one-third) of respondents who preferred a more immediate response needed to have their concerns addressed in some way.

At the time of the survey, NIU Libraries administration was investigating the possibility of launching a live chat reference service. The results of this survey on the Ask-A-Librarian service reflected a growing desire among some of the patrons for a more immediate response to their information needs. This informed the decision to proceed with chat software selection/purchase, and the pilot chat reference program began its planning phase. The Libraries purchased Docutek's VRLPlus software on a one-year trial basis. A major deciding factor in the selection of this product was the inclusion of an e-mail component. In VRLPlus, when a librarian is not available for live chat, it automatically points the patron to the online e-mail reference form. The Ask-A-Librarian coordinator can assign questions to specific librarians and transfer questions to other librarians for additional consultation. Questions and answers are stored on the Docutek system. All patrons' personal identifying information can be deleted, and answers can be edited for spelling, grammar, length, or content. Keywords can then be assigned to each pair of questions and answers, resulting in a searchable database of questions and answers that may be accessed by patrons and staff for future reference assistance. The VRLPlus software also automatically tracks statistics, allowing for customized statistical reports, and it features a survey construction component. Customized surveys may be built and stored for automatic distribution to patrons once they have utilized the service. All of these features aid in the soliciting and receipt of user feedback in an ongoing timely fashion, eliminating the need for separate analysis projects.

## CONCLUSION

Both the intended and unexpected results of this survey demonstrate how user satisfaction surveys can provide valuable information to libraries and librarians, particularly useful in the age of digital reference. Such assessment projects expose the strengths and weaknesses of current programs, pushing libraries to constantly analyze, improve, expand, and modify their service in all its forms of delivery. While not addressed in this article, evaluating the quality of the responses that are being delivered to patrons is also important. Evaluation of user satisfaction is really a first step in what should be a constant process of evaluation of all aspects of the service.

There are limitations to this or any user report-based measure of effectiveness. The evaluation of digital reference services itself would seem to indicate that the need for such services is assumed, and that the mode of delivery is sound. As well, user satisfaction survey participants are asked about their level of satisfaction with an existing service, not what else they want from their library or librarians. Feedback is gathered from a limited number of users, and by definition does not gather feedback from non-users. Perhaps the latter are not using a particular service because it does not adequately meet their needs. Future analyses need to examine this untapped population, to determine users' and non-users' perceptions of what they might be offered, and indeed to examine the assumption that the current modes of delivery of digital reference services are optimal.

Such research is needed, as there is little evidence in the literature that users are typically consulted in the design and development of digital reference. Rather, the development of digital reference services appears to be largely based on the interests and vision of service providers (Gross et al., 2003). Frequently, digital reference services replicate traditional reference services and models in the electronic realm without any indication that this meets users' needs. If academic libraries are serious about supporting the mission statements of their institutions, and are committed to implementing innovative services or achieving service excellence, they must include users in the planning and evaluation process.

Opportunities to improve service to users have been lost at many institutions by not involving users in the process in the planning stages, before a system or service was designed and implemented. Asking users how they see reference services, what they want from reference staff and collections, how they want reference information delivered, and how to best market reference services, will provide academic reference providers invaluable insight, and ultimately, practically, also save their institutions time and expense.

# REFERENCES

Bushallow-Wilbur, L., DeVinney, G., & Whitcomb, F. (1996). Electronic mail reference service: A study. *RQ, 35*, 359-371.

Diamond, W., & Pease, B. (2001). Digital reference: A case study of question types in an academic library. *Reference Services Review, 29* (3), 210-218.

Frank, I. (1998). E-mail reference at the University of South Florida: A well-kept secret. *Art Documentation, 17* (1), 8-9, 44-45.

Gray, S. M. (2000). Virtual reference services: Directions and agendas. *Reference & User Services Quarterly, 39* (4), 365-375.

Gross, M., McClure, C. R., & Lankes, R. D. (2003). Assessing quality in digital reference services: An overview of the key literature on digital reference. In R. D. Lankes, C. R. McClure, M. Gross, & J. Pomerantz (Eds.), *Implementing digital reference services: Setting standards and making it real.* New York: Neal-Schuman Publishers (pp. 171-183).

Horn, J., & Kjaer, K. (2000). Evaluating the "Ask a Question" service at the University of California, Irvine. In R. D. Lankes, J. W. Collins III, & A. S. Kasowitz (Eds.), *Digital reference service in the new millennium: Planning, management, and evaluation* (pp. 135-152). New York: Neal-Schuman Publishers.

Lankes, R. D. & Kasowitz, A. S. (1998). *The ask a starter kit: How to build and maintain digital reference services.* Syracuse, NY: ERIC Clearinghouse on Information & Technology. (ERIC Document Reproduction Service No. ED 427 779).

Lazar, J., & Preece, J. (1999). Designing and implementing web-based surveys. *Journal of Computer Information Systems, 39* (4), 63-67.

Lazar, J., & Preece, J. (2001). Using electronic surveys to evaluate networked resources: From idea to implementation. In C. R. McClure & J. C. Bertot (Eds.), *Evaluating networked information services: Techniques, policy, and issues* (pp. 137-154). Medford, New Jersey: Information Today.

Lederer, N. (2001). E-mail reference: Who, when, where, and what is asked. *The Reference Librarian, 74*, 55-73.

Powell, C. A., & Bradigan, P. S. (2001). E-mail reference services: Characteristics and effects on overall reference services at an academic health sciences library. *Reference & User Services Quarterly, 41* (2), 170-178.

Staley, L. A. (1998). E-mail reference: Experiences at City University. *PNLA Quarterly, 62* (4), 20-21.

Tomaiuolo, N. G., & Packer, J. G. (2000). AskA do's, don'ts, and how to's: Lessons learned in a library. *Searcher, 8* (3), 32-35.

Weissman, S.K. (2001). Considering a launch? *Library Journal, 126* (2), 49.

APPENDIX. Ask-A-Librarian User Satisfaction Survey Questionnaire

1. What was the main reason why you used "Ask a Librarian? Check all that apply

    a. for a undergraduate term paper
    b. for a graduate research paper
    c. for faculty research
    d. for technical help in using library resources
    e. for help in getting into a database
    f. other (specify)_____

2. Did you get the information that you needed?

    a. Yes      b. No

3. How prompt was the library response to your question?

    a. Very prompt–I had an answer within 24 hours
    b. Somewhat prompt–I had an answer within 48 hours (two days)
    c. Not too prompt–it took more than 48 hours
    d. I did not get a response. [Go to question 5.]

4. How helpful was the response you received?

    a. Very helpful
    b. Somewhat helpful
    c. Not too helpful
    d. Not helpful at all

5. Does having a response to your question within 48 hours meet your needs or do you need a quicker response time?

    a. Having a response within 48 hours is adequate for me.
    b. I need to have a response to my question more quickly.

6. How would you rate the "Ask the Librarian Service?"

    a. Excellent
    b. Good
    c. Only fair
    d. Poor

7. What suggestions do you have to improve the "Ask the Librarian" Service?

# How the GPO Got Its Groove Back: Government Printing Office and Government Information on the Internet

Kathy Hathaway

**SUMMARY.** In the last decade, the Government Printing Office has dealt with two major problems of this revolution. First, GPO has had to master the various aspects of the electronic age. Second, they have had to deal with the "under-the-gun" mentality of a government totally enamored of the "apparent" efficiency and accuracy of electronic information. GPO's struggle with these problems has been neither easy nor comfortable. From top to bottom in the government documents world nearly everyone has some degree of apprehension, misgiving, or outright suspicion concerning the future of the accessibility of government infor-

Kathy Hathaway is Government Documents Librarian, Poplar Creek Library, 1405 South Park Avenue, Streamwood, IL 60107 (E-mail: khathawa@poplarcreek.lib.il.us).

[Haworth co-indexing entry note]: "How the GPO Got Its Groove Back: Government Printing Office and Government Information on the Internet." Hathaway, Kathy. Co-published simultaneously in *The Reference Librarian* (The Haworth Information Press, an imprint of The Haworth Press, Inc.) No. 93, 2006, pp. 109-128; and: *New Directions in Reference* (ed: Byron Anderson, and Paul T. Webb) The Haworth Information Press, an imprint of The Haworth Press, Inc., 2006, pp. 109-128. Single or multiple copies of this article are available for a fee from The Haworth Document Delivery Service [1-800-HAWORTH, 9:00 a.m. - 5:00 p.m. (EST). E-mail address: docdelivery@haworthpress.com].

mation. Despite these difficulties GPO has made important strides toward implementing the apparatus of electronic information, while at the same time striving to ensure the quality and coherency of the end product available to the nation's citizens. *[Article copies available for a fee from The Haworth Document Delivery Service: 1-800-HAWORTH. E-mail address: <docdelivery@haworthpress.com> Website: <http://www.HaworthPress.com>*

**KEYWORDS.** Government Printing Office, government information, electronic products, dissemination of information on the Internet, archiving, preservation, Federal Documents Depository Program, Persistent Uniform Resource Locator, documents librarians

Rumor has it we are in an electronic revolution–a revolution in the collection, transmission, storage, and retrieval of information. As in any revolution, there are the pains of transition. In 2003, the Illinois government depository community began drafting a new state plan for the distribution and control of federal government documents, with the purpose of getting government information freely and accessibly to the people. This plan will be about as unlike its predecessor, drafted in 1991, as today's world of information and resulting knowledge is unlike the information world that existed before the advent of Internet dominance.

The state plan is intended to coordinate the Federal Documents Depository Program within a state, and to assist the regional depository libraries in each state in meeting their responsibilities to their member libraries and to the federal government. The idea of a state plan began in 1981 when the Depository Library Council of the Government Printing Office (GPO) passed a resolution recommending that the Public Printer investigate the feasibility of requiring each state to prepare a plan. The thought at the time was that state plans would be an efficient way to enable depository libraries to coordinate efforts to manage the rapidly growing government collection. This was in recognition of space and time constraints that challenged depository library mandates to provide quality service in getting government information to the population they served. At the time government information was in the form of physical, tangible documents, so manuals and guides for processing and disseminating this information was appropriate and sufficient. This is not the case anymore, and how this came to pass is an interesting story.

The Chief of the GPO's Library Programs Service's Depository Services, Robin Haun-Mohamed, stated, "The federal program is currently 66 percent electronic. There is a commitment to increase the mining of electronic material. There is still going to be a percentage of print (maps, large DVD format). Print is well on the way out."[1] Other sources have the goal of government publishing to be as much as 95 percent solely available in electronic format.[2] Federal government information will soon be available solely on the Internet, with the exception of certain large format material, and, probably, certain core documents of an official and archival nature that documents librarians hope will be around for a long time to come. The road to complete dissemination of government information on the Internet has been a rocky one, but surprisingly, not a particularly long one since the beginning.

In October 1995, Illinois librarians in attendance at the state's Documents Depository Librarians meeting became aware that government information, an environment with which they had been so familiar, and GPO, a trusted friend and confidante upon whom they have always relied, were undergoing a severe transition. There was a certain energized tone present at this meeting that bordered on anarchy, or the fear of it. John Shuler of the University of Illinois-Chicago had just recently returned from the GPO Depository Library Council meeting in Memphis, and he spoke at length and with portent about developments that occurred there. He stated that GPO was undergoing deep changes: the federal government was in favor of electronic access for most documents and was going ahead with this. This was the first time that GPO had ever been ahead of the documents community on information issues. Moreover, depository libraries were to be on their own with these changes; it would be up to the librarians to provide meaningful access to CD-ROM products and Internet sources. Shuler also wondered whether, in the end-stage of electronic transition, GPO would still be necessary, and indeed, would there still be a need for depository libraries?[3]

There were pressing and specific concerns that besieged documents librarians at the time. First, as documents became available only through the Internet, librarians realized that they did not actually have the documents, at least until downloaded. Second, librarians realized that they must find the documents first; and before that, must find out about them. Third, many librarians realized that things may not stay on the Internet indefinitely, and that they have no control over the longevity of a document at a particular site. Other questions asked were, Will agencies archive? Will the National Archives become involved? Coming back to the problem of discovery and access, how will "older" documents be secured that were not originally discovered and accessed? Should librarians "grab" everything found on the Internet, or should they feel secure that what is needed will be at a documented site for future access? This would change how depository libraries "index" available information, since they would not physically hold the documents in this scenario. Of course, all of this presupposes archiving by the source or a centralized entity like the National Archives. What about source confirmation? When Internet searchers find what is wanted, will they be able to identify and confirm the source and be scrupulous about doing this? In other words, is a specific agency report actually from the agency, or is it someone just commenting on it?

Finally, when everything is solely available on the Internet, do we logically conclude that depository libraries will cease to exist? This is not as much a reflection of self-preserving paranoia as it may seem. Will the very basis of free access to government information, so crucial to a democratic society, be compromised? It must be understood that in the 1995 atmosphere of the Internet run amok, these were very legitimate worries. The Internet at the time was an extremely unrestrained and unmanageable animal; no significant amount of order was imposed upon it. Even today, some things have not changed, but thanks to GPO, in just two years, the Internet has a meaningful mode to accessing government information. There has been significant improvement to realize the government's initial goal of getting the documents to the people, and to every person's computer, simultaneously and efficiently.

In contrast to the atmosphere at the Illinois State Depository meeting in 1995, the tone of the 1998 Federal Depository Conference in Washington, DC, was congenial and reassuring to the hundreds of depository librarians who were hosted. Discussion at this conference, along with sessions of GPO's Depository Library Council, were awash with talk of agency cooperation, GPO fighting for depository access to previously inaccessible sources, and the Persistent Uniform Resource Locator (PURL), explained below. The discussion envisioned the relationship between GPO and depository libraries as each performing their appropriate role to fulfill the mission of getting government information to the citizenry. The Depository Library Council would act as a liaison between the two entities–the depository libraries and the Government Printing Office. As depository librarians, themselves, Council members could clearly express the need for GPO to gain control of electronic documents and get them to depository libraries, just as they had done with paper products in the past. Depository libraries must do the job they are charged with: get the end product–government information–to the people they serve in any fashion or format that is necessary to achieve this goal. At the same time, the Depository Library Council members were delegated to make depository libraries understand that GPO operates under a financial constraint. By this time, GPO's struggle with Congress over its budget had become legendary; they had even been threatened with no budget whatsoever. To paraphrase some Congressional views, "What do we need a government printing office for, if all government documents are going to be coming into everyone's home via the Internet?" Admittedly, GPO's self-preservation fears have been based in reality.

An earlier conference featured how government information was going to be disseminated on the Internet. In 1997, the Fifth North Carolina Serials Conference, Burlington, North Carolina, identified three areas of concern involving government documents and the Internet: archiving Internet sources, cataloging Internet sources, and the future of the Federal Depository Library Program. Here, again, the question of whether GPO would continue to exist, or if it even needed to exist, hung over the conference. The conference was attended and moderated by "folks" with keen interest on government information issues–academic librarians with the responsibility of a government depository. One topic of interest was PURL (Persistent Uniform Resource Locator), a cataloging device designed to redirect the user to an operative Internet site from a Web site no longer active. Used in the 856 cataloging field to provide a target Internet address for a specific document, PURL acts as a permanent address for an item. GPO had been working with OCLC on the problem of broken links. GPO, via PURL, would update a broken URL by going back to the current Web site of the agency for the document. The effort was more than a cataloging issue: it addressed the issue of permanency, authenticity, and to a certain extent, archiving of electronic government documents. These are crucial issues, then and now, to public accessibility of government information. Moreover, PURL assures accessibility to particular government documents at authentic, certified government Web sites that get the actual government report from the originating source. At the 1998 Federal Depository Conference in Washington, DC, the GPO was ready to reveal that PURLs were a reality. The question posed at the North Carolina conference, "who better to provide a centralized location for this task?" had its answer, "no one better than the Government Printing Office." GPO finds it, identifies it, catalogs it, and provides permanent access to the specific, authentic document that an informed public needs and wants. The question of whether or not GPO would still be around in a couple of years had its answer–no agency or entity was better qualified to meet this permanent access need as efficiently and cheaply as the GPO, and they proved it.

From the chaos of 1995 to its emerging role as the one source to go to for government information on the Internet, GPO had learned in this untested environment to approach issues from an inventive perspective. This was achieved in a few scant years. In addition to the astonishingly quick development of its own laudable Web site, GPO Access, it became clear that GPO was also in the business of forging new friendships. In December 1997, GPO signed an Interagency Agreement with the Department of Energy creating the DOE Information Bridge. Whereas documents librarians had previously focused on GPO Access as the solitary access point to the government's electronic collection, a new understanding became generally accepted that multiple approaches must be used to gain access to the information. With this understanding, GPO set its sights on the whole world of electronic government information.

At the 1998 Washington meeting, Gil Baldwin of the Library Program Services of GPO informed attendees that the Federal Depository Library Program Electronic Collection was comprised of four elements: core regulatory and legislative products that are permanently managed by GPO Access; GPO remotely accessible products, still managed primarily by GPO; tangible electronic products distributed through the depository system; and remotely accessible electronic products issued and controlled by the originating agencies that GPO identifies and links to. At the time, this signified a subtle, but significant, departure from the long held belief that GPO must control the entire government information collection. This was something that, actually, had never been possible, even before the "infestation" of electronic products. It could be that issues raised by the proliferation of electronic government information had forced the hand of the principals involved. Being unable to get control of agency electronic products had perhaps forced GPO to figure out how to establish meaningful cooperation with the agencies. With the advent of the 1997 DOE Information Bridge, GPO set the stage for new interagency cooperation, often characterized by formal agreements with other government agencies. This allowed freer access to agency publications that had never before been available to the public at large. With the DOE Information Bridge, 25,000 DOE research reports became available through GPO Access, and all, or most, recent reports issued from the Department of Energy's Office of Scientific and Technical Information could be gotten directly from the GPO Access and DOE Information Bridge Web sites. These reports were primarily DOE funded research and development products from 1996 on, and current reports were added daily as they were issued. Some of these reports had previously been distributed only selectively to depository libraries in microfiche, which had always been subject to microfiche contractor and backlog woes. This was the first attempt to allow the public meaningful access to these reports. Other agencies, like the Department of Interior, were expected to enter into similar agreements with GPO. Although, at the time, statutory language allowed agencies to exclude electronic products from the depository system, the new cooperative attitudes were resulting in better access to "fugitive-classed" documents.

Closely mirroring Interagency Agreements were pilot projects and new legislation that would give documents librarians electronic access to government sources that had inadequate or no access to in the past, notably three popular and sought-after sources: National Technical Information Service (NTIS), Educational Resources Information Center (ERIC), and Congressional Research Service (CRS) publications. The NTIS/GPO Electronic Image Format Pilot Project, that involved at least twenty-four institutions, promised to provide depository access to NTIS electronic publications. NTIS publications are technical reports funded by the government, but available only through sale by that agency. Long a source of argument between the depository library community and government agencies, current NTIS documents would now be available free of charge to depository libraries, and through us, to the public. The Federal Depository Library Project's ERIC Digital Library Pilot Project would assure electronic access to federally-funded ERIC reports that were in the public domain. Depository libraries had previously had access to these reports only in microfiche. It was proposed that by July 1998, the 300 libraries in the pilot group would have electronic access to ERIC reports from 1997 forward; all depository libraries would have access by late 1998. At the time, there were two bills in Congress that would get depository access to electronic CRS publications. While these had been online for some time, neither depository libraries, nor the public could gain access to them. Congressional legislation, if passed, would finally grant access to these elusive, but extremely popular publications. Unfortunately, as of mid-2003, none of these projects had been fully realized.

In a scant few years, the Government Printing Office had grasped seemingly insurmountable issues concerning dissemination of government information on the Internet. GPO had faced and weathered severe budget constraints, and came to grips with the possibility, and even probability, of its own cessation. GPO continued to live up to its responsibilities to the depository library community, and through them, deliver government information to the people. By the time of the 1998 Federal Depository Conference in Washington, DC, GPO had met every challenge put to it, with the exception of archiving, a moot point among GPO, the National Archives, and the agencies themselves. What new issues do GPO and depository libraries face as they move from the world of government information on the Internet to a world where government information is available *solely* on the Internet, especially without a safety net?

## ARCHIVING AND PERMANENT ACCESS TO ELECTRONIC INFORMATION

If Federal government agencies are going to have sole responsibility for placing their important publications electronically on the agencies' Web sites, and if there is to be no other format given to GPO to handle and preserve, the issue of the longevity of that information comes into question. Who is going to guarantee that these publications are going to be permanently available from that agency, and that important information generated by that government agency is going to be preserved? Does GPO plan on continuing and expanding its role in electronic preservation? And how will this be done? The GPO recently entered into a compact with the Office of Management and Budget (OMB) that will "allow Federal agencies direct access to printing vendors for the purpose of placing printing orders, while at the same time enabling the GPO to meet its statutory requirements."[4] With this agreement, OMB and GPO hope to reduce the cost of Federal printing, while enabling increased assurance of permanent public access to all non-classified government publications. Vendors wishing to participate in this contract would pledge to provide their "most favored customer pricing" to Federal customers and would be required to provide GPO with one electronic version and two paper copies of every document ordered under this contract. The Superintendent of Documents will continue to have access to these publications to produce for public distribution at its own expense. Robin Haun-Mohamed, Chief of GPO's Depository Services' Library Programs Service, had this to say:

> GPO is committed to continuing its role in electronic preservation. In the past, with a tangible collection, preservation of the collection was distributed to the libraries in the FDLP, located in Con-

gressional Districts across the country. With the development of the electronic collection, GPO can no longer rely on this very large and mostly stable preservation system done by the local libraries. Electronic resources must be refreshed and sometimes reformatted to ensure continued access to the resources in the future. GPO has asked for funds to update the GPO Access system, to bring the resources out of the WAIS-based system and into the next generation software. This is something GPO is committed to doing to ensure future public access. GPO is also working with NARA to establish GPO as an electronic affiliate, that is, the GPO Access databases are the official record copies, and these will be held at GPO, not transferred to NARA.[5] Documents librarians hope to expand this discussion to include other online and tangible electronic products beyond the GPO Access databases.

GPO has been instrumental in developing the Permanent Public Access (PPA) working group that cut across agencies' lines to review and address issues associated with public access to electronic resources. Other projects in which GPO is working to ensure future access to electronic information include the LOCKSS (Lots Of Copies Keep Stuff Safe) project, the OCLC pilot project for Web harvesting and archiving of electronic resources, and working with some in the depository community to identify, refresh/reformat information sent out to libraries on CD-ROMs which run on platforms that are no longer standard. Our commitment to long-term preservation is evident in these projects.

The new compact with OMB and GPO is a win-win situation for all. It allows for the provision of publications, as established in Title 44, and yet allows much greater flexibility and control by the agency over local printing decisions. The test agency chosen by OMB is the Department of Labor. GPO will certify a number of contractors to provide printing services for DOL. Labor will then choose the contractor they wish to use, and the contractor is responsible for providing information to GPO to allow the Superintendent of Documents to 'ride' the agency order to acquire depository and/or sales copies. In addition, the contractor is to provide an electronic file, in a format chosen by the Superintendent of Documents, and two paper copies of each publication produced under the agreement. The beauty of this agreement is the inclusion of a provision that the contractor is not paid until these materials are received and certified by the Superintendent of Documents. This allows all parties to abide by the regulations set forth in Title 44, and yet provides greater flexibility for the publishing agency. The project is set to start in Octo-

ber and additional information will be provided as the project pro-
gresses, but we are very excited about the future potential of this
process.

As far as a rewrite of the 44 USC §1901-1916, there are many areas
that are in need of updating, especially with regard to how a publication
is defined and the continued reliance on printing, but a total rewrite will
be difficult to bring about. The OMB project allows us to bring new
ideas into publishing and ways to include products in the FDLP that do
not require the extensive work that would be needed in rewrite.[6]

## DISPERSAL OF GOVERNMENT INFORMATION

People researching specific topics are used to perusing favorite government serials for the information they need. Sometimes, as these become available only on the Web, information and data in them get
dispersed in several different places, thereby challenging the identity of
the source, and diminishing its usefulness as a browsable research aid.
With this kind of dispersal, the quality of information must be scruti-
nized when a title goes electronic. Even from what is considered to be
very reliable government Internet sources, it is sometimes possible to
access only parts of tables or statistics, whereas the previous hard copy
always included full tables and data, including methodology and other
information used for gathering data, all accessible and capable of being
browsed within the book. Electronic sources have the tendency to lead
to information, rather than reliable publications that can be used to put
information in a frame of reference, as well as elucidate and analyze dis-
crete bits of material. As government agencies become more independent of publishing Web serials, how will agencies be alerted and informed
of these publications and sets of data? Mike Ragen, Chief Deputy Director of the Illinois State Library, had this to say:

> That is a difficult scramble for GPO and the State Library as well.
> This is the modern version of the "fugitive" documents issue we
> have all been struggling with through the years. Agencies need to
> be educated about the problems with independent dispersal of doc-
> uments as well. The reason we have libraries is for the uniform
> collection and dispersal of information. People know to go to a li-
> brary for information. If agencies don't go through the depository
> process, their documents are useless. These documents become
> one of billions of free-floating web pages that crowd the Internet.

Depositories can help agencies get their message delivered. This is important because if the taxpayers don't know what an agency does, or know how to access the agency's information, the agency is worthless to the public and a waste of taxpayer dollars.[7]

Robin Haun-Mohamed had these comments:

> Early on we noticed how agencies dispersed serials throughout many different Web pages. Some even had you put together the serial publication (pull some from this page and another part from that page, and add it together and voila, you have a close resemblance to the paper product). Agencies have improved their organizational patterns from the early days, but serials still continue to be time intensive to identify the new issues and track the name changes. In a recent serials conference, many people agreed that serials will continue to take much of the time devoted to bibliographic control and authority work.
>
> GPO will continue to work with agencies, through the Federal Publishers Committee and other organizations to put forth best practices for serial publications. We are looking at developing Web pages to pull the various serials together to assist patrons and librarians in identifying the most recent resources. But in considering this option, we must be careful to allow for authenticity and agency control over their publications. This is very much an idea for the future. Another idea is to develop procedures to push cataloging records of serial titles to the libraries, including records for specific issues that we have not provided information in the Catalog of Government Publications in the past.[8]

## NATIONAL SECURITY
### versus FREEDOM OF INFORMATION

The national security issue versus an informed populace is forever a timely topic, but challenges to freedom of information in the world of electronic government information may take on different aspects of the same challenges that have historically been present. Mike Ragen expressed his opinion on this:

> In the past, in the primarily paper-based society, maintaining secure documents was a relatively easy task. We simply had locked

file cabinets with guards and limited access. The public had little or no access to documents or information that was useful or vital to the public. There were few legal rights to obtain such information. An example of that are the environmental records and weapons testing records that were protected for many years. People exposed to hazardous chemicals could not obtain the information or were even informed of the existence of such information. Today is a different story. On the state and federal level there are freedom of information laws that allow for public access to documents. Even those that are protected from disclosure can be subjected to judicial review.

Today there is so much information available that the public can easily be confused as to what to believe. There is the problem of sabotage of government web documents by hackers. Additionally, with terrorism plaguing our society there is a need to protect information that could jeopardize the health and safety of millions of citizens. Information management is a very difficult job today. A sensitive document can easily be transmitted on a global basis in seconds. Balancing the public right to know with public safety is a huge responsibility for our government agencies. Given that there is a formal judicial process for obtaining secure documents, I must weigh in as being overly cautious on making some types of documents publicly available, especially those involving public safety, for example, the public water supply CD-ROM that was withdrawn by the GPO. This is a whole new territory for our society and our culture. We must proceed carefully.[9]

Robin Haun-Mohamed had this to add:

The issue of national security is more visible that it has ever been before. In the past when tangible materials were distributed, it was easier to make a recall and be relatively sure that materials were retrieved. In an electronic environment it is more difficult because the copies are not tangible, but copies may have been downloaded and printed out in libraries and from other computers. It is not possible to account for all the copies in a recall. In some views, this is a good thing, because information will continue to be available even the files may have been pulled from a Web site. The challenge is to find a way to save the material from disappearing completely, so that it can then be made available in a future time when security restrictions no longer apply to the specific document. This is another area in which GPO is hoping to open discussions with NARA to ensure these materials remain available in some format, that hopefully can be made available in the future.[10]

## GOVERNMENT INFORMATION AND PUBLIC LIBRARIES

Librarians are the virtual inventors of the pathfinder, the guide, and the bibliography that lead people to their goal. In addition, they are capable of educating users about the sources therein. If all government information will soon be available on the Internet, and no other place, it is logical to assume that all public and non-depository librarians will be expected to provide the expertise needed to access and understand government information. The question of how GPO and depository libraries will help users is a pertinent one. Mike Ragen responded:

> As with any institution, GPO has limitations and asking them to reach out to all the public libraries is an expansion of duties they can't achieve under the current budget constraints. At our recent Illinois Government Depository Library conference held at the State Library, we had a very good discussion on this issue. We believe the State Library and the selective depositories can play an important role in expanding the public awareness of the availability and usefulness of government documents. Local outreach works best. Illinois is fortunate to have a strong network of depository libraries, both on the academic level and in public libraries. In the next few months the depository community will be making a move towards promoting document access and assistance on a statewide basis.[11]

Robin Haun-Mohamed devoted a great deal of time to this subject:

> This is an excellent question, especially in light of recent efforts by the Superintendent of Documents, Judith C. Russell, and the Public Printer, Bruce James, to reach out to those in the FDLP library community and those outside the community, to help envision the future of government information dissemination. This discussion began with the spring 2003 meeting of the Depository Library Council, when Mr. James challenged the community to reinvent information dissemination to the general public in light of the 21st

Century. The discussion has continued since the April meeting, with outreach efforts to law, medical, academic, regional, and public libraries. In discussions with the Public Library Association and the Urban Library Council, GPO has raised the issue of one size not fitting all–that is the Basic Collection (or core resources) for a public library may not be the same as the Basic Collection for an academic or law library. There is a strongly held assumption that most citizens will not think first of visiting an academic library for government information, but rather that the public library is the more natural place for inquiries. With far fewer public libraries in the program (about 20% are public libraries and 50% academic), it is important to increase the number of access points in public libraries. One approach is to increase outreach to public libraries, to bring more libraries into the FDLP. In addition, consideration is being given to developing government information service centers, outside the auspices of the formal program of the FDLP. Staff in these service areas would be provided a minimal amount of training, to allow staff to answer basic reference questions and train staff to make referrals to neighboring depository libraries as appropriate. We are hoping to develop a certification process, perhaps in coordination with PLA, that would make this process attractive to new depository libraries. Another idea for reaching outside the depository community is to increase the visibility of government information in school and media center libraries. One way to do this is develop a core collection of resources, such as the Statistical Abstract, the U.S. Government Manual, and a few other titles, that would be provided to these libraries to help ensure broader access and familiarity with Federal government information products in non-FDLP libraries. All of these ideas, brought forth in recent discussion with the Superintendent of Documents and GPO staff on recent library visits and telephone discussions, build upon the knowledge and expertise found in the network of Federal depository libraries already in place. We look forward to continuing these discussions in the near future, including sessions scheduled for the Fall 2003 Federal Depository Library Council.[12]

Finally and overall, how do we assess GPO's performance in aiding depository libraries with the transition to electronic dissemination? Mike Ragen:

I like the direction GPO is going right now. They, like everyone else, are struggling with the electronic environment. I think they are doing a good job in advising depositories on the electronic dissemination of documents. Our whole culture is still in the transition period of moving from a paper-based society to the electronic environment. The Federal government is a huge enterprise, generating nearly 30,000 documents per year from numerous large and complex agencies. GPO staff is doing the best they can given the limits that are imposed upon them. Agencies don't always cooperate with GPO, so they must deal with that bureaucratic aspect of life.[13]

Robin Haun-Mohamed:

Since Congress began directing GPO to move to a mostly electronic Federal Depository Library Program (FDLP), GPO has been providing assistance to depository libraries to help with the transition. This help included developing workstation specifications for public access workstations and these are updated each year. Guidelines have been developed to assist the depository community in forming policies and procedures for electronic services and even more specifically, for Internet services. GPO has worked with agencies to increase and improve the number of electronic products available through the FDLP. In coordination with OCLC, GPO put into place a program to uniquely identify and allow changes to be more easily made to online resources by utilizing the Persistent Uniform Resource Locator (PURL) naming process. These PURLS have been included in the GPO cataloging records for many years.

Other areas in which GPO has provided assistance to libraries in the electronic transition has been an increased emphasis on agency training, including the GPO Access Databases. In coordination with STAT-USA, additional training has been included under the GPO Access training program. The Depository Library Conference and Council Meeting, held each fall in Washington, DC routinely includes program and sessions dealing with electronic resources. The spring Depository Library Council Meeting, held in a different area of the country each spring also includes training opportunities. Conference proceedings for many of these training sessions are available from the FDLP Desktop.

Future projections to continue with the transition to a mostly electronic FDLP included agency outreach to work on formats and proprietary software associated with tangible electronic products. A best practices approach is being taken in information exchanges with agency publishers and Web masters whenever possible. GPO personnel also continue to work with the congressional staff members to advise on the status of electronic transition in the libraries, and provide feedback to staff based on the responses GPO hears from the depository community.[14]

Depository librarians display definite skills when it comes to gaining access to government publications and information. Looking to the future, depository librarians need to ask how they got these skills and how these skills will evolve. At the Fifth North Carolina Serials Conference in 1997, John Shuler pointed out that "all the tools of the electronic age are not going to make you have more information, they're going to make you have less."[15] He also spoke highly of public libraries and their mission to provide free information to a democratic society. He urged academic libraries to pursue this ideal. He expressed confidence in public librarianship, and the ability of any librarian to learn how to navigate his or her way around governmental Internet sites. Would this really happen, or would something be lost? Depository librarians are well versed in the organization of government agencies, and knowledgeable when it comes to the workings of Congress, for example, how laws get passed and in what manner. Where did this expertise come from? Experience, mostly learned on the job. Librarians have had the help and support of the Federal Depository Library Program and GPO, but when it came to finding their way around government documents, librarians were pretty much on their own. By the same token, couldn't any public librarian become knowledgeable about government information? When it comes to government information on the Internet, documents librarians are dealing with a completely new format, so the playing field is somewhat leveled. Documents librarians have always had help from each other, that is, knowledge passed down from one expert to the next. This type of training cannot easily be replaced. Will public librarians be able to learn this on their own and use it to navigate the new sources for government information on the Internet? Yes, but it will be difficult to do without help. Whether or not depository libraries continue to exist officially, the experience of documents librarians will still be needed, and they will continue to help one another. Any state wishing to adopt a current state plan for its depository libraries, especially those that realistically expect to overcome new and serious challenges of free access to government information on the Internet, must not fail to recognize and use the untapped value that is inherent in public, non-depository libraries.

GPO worries about libraries leaving the depository library program. Libraries seem to be making this decision on their own without getting any input from document coordinators. GPO has put together a Web page entitled, "Stay with the Program," listing reasons that libraries should remain in the Federal Depository Library Program. Above all, GPO urges depository libraries to contact GPO before making the final decision to relinquish depository status. In her article, "Dealing with Digital," Marylaine Block interviewed Chuck Malone of Western Illinois University, who had a somewhat different view of the topic. Malone said, "I really see a future where with more and more government information online, and more shared online OPACs, just about any library can be a government information library, regardless of whether they participate in the FDLP. Then those that remain in the FDLP can serve a consulting and coordinating role to assist the non-depositories."[16] Other document librarians she interviewed worried more about the future of their profession, but still held "several truths to be self-evident." "The more power the government has, the more essential it is that it be held accountable for its actions. Information is the sunlight that exposed slimy crawling things like incompetence and corruption and sends them running for cover. And, most importantly, the mission of depository librarians is to provide that sun."[17] Haun-Mohamed had this to add about what libraries had to offer in the new world of government information:

> What do libraries bring to the FDLP in the (electronic) transition? So many things. This is truly a partnership, especially as people continue to participate in the program, when so much is now available free on the Internet. We know that not "everything" is available on the Internet, but much that is current use is. So why remain a part of the FDLP–I think we have done a good job in pulling together ideas from the "Stay with the Program" page available from the desktop. Other things the libraries bring–help with identification of electronic resources, continued maintenance and transitioning of the tangible collection, and most importantly the expertise available from the librarians in the depository community. Libraries are a public good–I believe this, and good people help our citizens gain access to the resources and help following the activities of their government.[18]

As a cautionary note regarding information and the Internet in general, Clifford Stoll, himself one of the pioneers of the Internet and one of its most insightful critics, said:

> But the Internet, for all its promise, doesn't deliver much information–it's mainly a data highway. Data isn't information. . . . Information, unlike data, has accuracy. It's reliable. It's timely. Understandable. . . . Information, unlike data, is useful. While there's a gulf between data and information, there's a wide ocean between information and knowledge. What turns the gears in our brains isn't information, but ideas, inventions, and inspiration. Knowledge–not information–implies understanding. And beyond knowledge lies what we should be seeking: wisdom. Sadly, our information society values data over experience, maturity, compassion, and enlightenment.[19]

In her article, Marylaine Block has an anecdote to relate from Chuck Malone:

> The story Malone most likes to tell, though, is about an older man who browsed the military collection while waiting for help with an obscure tax form. When Malone returned with his tax information, the man had tears in his eyes. Fifty-one years earlier in Korea, he told Malone, he and his unit were ordered to march to a hill where they fought for four days, then abruptly were ordered to return to where they started. His best friends had died there, but until he read an account of that battle in a book Malone had led him to, he had no idea what the point was, or whether they had accomplished anything.[20]

Government information is diverse, and comes in many forms and formats. Given the less than browsable nature of the Internet, it's unlikely that this piece of information would have been available to that fortuitous patron, paging through one of the government's notable military history sets. Documents librarians can only hope that there will always be a place that can house these valuable archival documents, and that there will always be a place in our government's plan for depository libraries. John Shuler, at the 1997 Illinois Initiative Conference in Peoria that concentrated on citizen education, noted, "I envision a world where only one official document of some government information will be produced and held at just one location, allowing access to virtually no one, while various portions and versions of the document will float around the Internet at so-called 'official' government sites."[21] At least GPO, with its commitment to the actual publication, has helped preserve the identity of the document online; however, this is somewhat analogous to a finger in the dike. Much could be lost if librarians have to rely on the Internet being the sole holder of government information, knowledge and wisdom. A quote from an anonymous source sums up the difficult transition to government information in electronic format:

> The past decade has seen the Government Printing Office dramatically shift its focus to the collection and retention of electronic information. It would seem that this shift from hard copy to electronic copy was in the way of self-preservation. The dictates of budget ultimatums may have left the agency with no realistic alternatives. But. But survival through this decade of change should not be viewed as a victory. The goal of the GPO is not truly the printing/saving or archiving of government agencies' information. The purpose is really to provide access to as much government information as possible within the most narrow restraints of national security as possible to as many citizens as possible in the most convenient ways possible. These are the ramparts the GPO and the Federal Depository Libraries must be manning. Somewhere in Mr. Smith's America there is a whistle-blower about to discover the truth concerning Willet Creek, and it could be that the only way he or she will be able to do that is through information provided by the GPO. In the free and open democracy we wish to preserve that information is crucial. There is no excuse for betraying the government's obligation to be as open as possible with the electorate that government serves. We spend far too much money to claim lack of funds. In truth, the Internet should just be one more way for a citizen to find information; it should never, never, ever be the only way. The possible abuses, to say nothing of innocent difficulties, of electronic data storage and retrieval, should frighten any intelligent citizen. The difficulties of modern democracy are legion. Claiming that economy or practicality dictates the move to the Internet might be an easy answer to this struggle. It is the wrong answer. A government born of the consent of the governed has an obligation, regardless of cost, to be transparent. Open and easy access to government activity and information in as many formats as possible is a crucial issue and should be treated as an important component in the defense of this Nation.

The heroes of a free society fight daily against the entropic powers of bureaucracy, apathy, and a host of nameless plagues. The burdens that GPO shoulders has bent them but not broken them. They are heroes. They should stay the course. The GPO, through libraries, will continue to illuminate the government to the people.

## NOTES

1. Robin Haun-Mohammed, interview by author, correspondence, July 2003.
2. Marylaine Block, "Dealing with Digital," *Library Journal* 128, no. 12 (2003), 40.
3. John Shuler, contribution to the Illinois Documents Depository Librarians Meeting, Illinois State Library, Springfield, (October 27, 1995).
4. "GPO and OMB Announce a New Compact for Government Printing," *GPO News Release*, June 6, 2003, http://www.gpo.gov/public-affairs/news/03news27.pdf.
5. On August 12, 2003, GPO announced that they have officially signed this agreement with the National Archives. In their Web site news release entitlee, "GPO and National Archives Unite in Support of Permanent Online Public Access," GPO stated that this agreement " . . . sets a framework for collaboration between the two agencies that will ensure that documents available today on GPO Access will remain available permanently."
6. Robin Haun-Mohamed, interview by author.
7. Mike Regan, interview by author, correspondence, July 2003.
8. Robin Haun-Mohamed, interview by author.
9. Mike Ragen, interview by author.
10. Robin Haun-Mohamed, interview by author.
11. Mike Regan, interview by author.
12. Robin Haun-Mohamed, interview by author.
13. Mike Regan, interview by author.
14. Robin Haun-Mohamed, interview by author.
15. John Shuler, "New Issues Facing Serials/Documents Librarians," keynote address, Fifth North Carolina Serials Conference, Burlington, NC, April 4-6, 1997.
16. Block, "Dealing with Digital," 43.
17. Ibid.
18. Robin Haun-Mohamed, interview by author.
19. Clifford Stoll, *High Tech Heretic: Why Computers Don't Belong in the Classroom and Other Reflections by a Computer Contrarian* (New York: Doubleday, 1999): 186.
20. Block, "Dealing with Digital," 41.
21. John Shuler, "Citizen Education," Illinois Initiative Conference workshop, Peoria, Illinois, July 27, 1997.

# Golden Rule Reference:
# Face-to-Face and Virtual

Chad E. Buckley

**SUMMARY.** Reference service in all types of libraries could be improved if librarians actively adopted the mindset of the Golden Rule. The Rule is expressed in some form in many world religions and instructs us to treat others how we would like to be treated. This approach has applicability not only in face-to-face reference transactions, but also in virtual reference. The empathetic reference librarian should be alert to both verbal and non-verbal clues that can indicate how a patron would like to be treated. *[Article copies available for a fee from The Haworth Document Delivery Service: 1-800-HAWORTH. E-mail address: <docdelivery@haworthpress.com> Website: <http://www.HaworthPress.com> © 2006 by The Haworth Press, Inc. All rights reserved.]*

**KEYWORDS.** Golden Rule, reference service, patron treatment, reference transactions, virtual reference

Imagine for a moment that you are a patron approaching a reference desk in a library, or in this age of virtual 24/7 reference that you are initi-

Chad E. Buckley is Science Reference Librarian, Milner Library, Illinois State University, Normal, IL 61790 (E-mail: cebuckle@ilstu.edu).

[Haworth co-indexing entry note]: "Golden Rule Reference: Face-to-Face and Virtual." Buckley, Chad E. Co-published simultaneously in *The Reference Librarian* (The Haworth Information Press, an imprint of The Haworth Press, Inc.) No. 93, 2006, pp. 129-136; and: *New Directions in Reference* (ed: Byron Anderson, and Paul T. Webb) The Haworth Information Press, an imprint of The Haworth Press, Inc., 2006, pp. 129-136. Single or multiple copies of this article are available for a fee from The Haworth Document Delivery Service [1-800-HAWORTH, 9:00 a.m. - 5:00 p.m. (EST). E-mail address: docdelivery@haworthpress.com].

doi:10.1300/J120v45n93_10

ating a chat reference session or sending an e-mail query to a librarian. Just what is it that you expect from this encounter? Do you hope for just a reasonably correct answer? Or do you also expect that the librarian will be both helpful and respectful? Do you have other expectations, perhaps related to the promptness of the librarian's reply or the form that the information you receive will take? The answers to these unspoken questions in a patron's mind go a long way toward determining whether they perceive they are receiving good service.

Many attempts have been made over the years to improve reference service. Our attention has been directed toward the importance of the reference interview, the poor accuracy rate of answers to reference queries, and concepts such as tiered reference. Recently, Miller stated that "there is nothing wrong with reference that common sense and the Golden Rule cannot cure."[1] However, he did not really elaborate on this idea. What exactly would reference service be like if librarians actually applied the Golden Rule on a day-to-day basis? Perhaps if we can further articulate what common sense tells us and examine in-depth the concept of the Golden Rule, this might give us an idea of additional ways to improve reference service, both in person and virtual.

Most librarians learned in library school that their behavior has some influence on reference transactions. Interpersonal communication, both verbal and nonverbal, is very important in the reference encounter. This knowledge, however, does not always translate into the type of service that patrons expect. As Miller suggested, keeping a simple principle in the forefront of our minds can help in this regard. It is not so much that we do not know how to provide good reference service, but that by adopting the mindset of the Golden Rule, we can more intuitively do so regardless of the circumstances before us. An honest attempt to apply the Golden Rule in reference encounters can greatly enhance the quality of service provided to patrons and can benefit any type of library.

Everyone has at one time or another heard the aphorism encouraging one "to put yourself in someone else's shoes." Such a comment is typically made to promote empathy and is essentially another way of stating the Golden Rule. The reference desk, whether physical or virtual, is one setting where the application of this saying is particularly apropos since librarianship is essentially a service profession and therefore focused on the needs of patrons. As reference librarians, we may have our own professional and personal goals for a reference encounter, but the patron's needs should remain paramount in our minds.

The Golden Rule basically states, "Do unto others as you would have them do unto you." It is found in some form in many world religions, including Judaism, Christianity, Islam, Hinduism, Buddhism, and Confucianism.[2] Wattles sums up the Golden Rule thusly, "What could be easier to grasp intuitively than the golden rule? . . . I know how I like to be treated; and that is how I am to treat others. The rule asks me to be considerate of others rather than indulging in self-centeredness."[3] The Rule may also be stated in a negative version which urges that you *not* do to others what you would *not* like done to you. It does not, as some think, suggest that one "Do unto others *as* they do unto you." This implies vengeance and retaliation that are antithetical to the true spirit of the Rule. Nor does the Golden Rule implore that we treat others in the manner in which *they* would like, for we cannot easily know exactly how they would wish to be treated. We do know how we might wish to be treated in a similar situation.

With regard to reference service in libraries, the issue then becomes how would we personally like to be treated in a reference encounter? One can make some generalizations that would likely apply to the majority of encounters with patrons. However, specifics will vary from patron to patron, and our task as reference librarians is to use whatever clues are available to discern the patron's circumstances and then empathize how we might like to be treated in those particular circumstances, to put ourselves in their shoes as it were.

General behavioral characteristics of effective reference encounters are well summarized in a 1996 RASD document.[4] These guidelines cover much of the generally courteous behavior that is to be expected from reference librarians in a physical reference desk setting and include specific behaviors related to approachability, interest, listening, searching and follow-up. Many of these behaviors could be considered "common sense" as suggested by Miller, and if we would typically expect to be treated in such a manner, we can assume that most other patrons would also.

Picture the following scenario in a library. You, the patron, walk up to a reference desk where a librarian is earnestly working at a computer. You stand and wait for several minutes before the librarian offers to help you. During that time the librarian never even acknowledges your presence by saying they will be with you shortly. Or if the librarian does help you immediately, they are brusque and never smile or make eye contact. Such a librarian is obviously failing to exhibit approachability or to display interest or listening. The RASD Guidelines adequately address most general situations such as these.

These guidelines can also be easily transferred to the virtual reference environment. Just as one should be responsive when a patron approaches a physical reference desk, so the virtual librarian ought to quickly reply to an e-mail query or promptly greet a patron who has begun a chat reference session. Timely assistance remains imperative, just as in face-to-face reference transactions. We all appreciate not being made to wait any longer than necessary. Another important issue related to the concept of virtual approachability is that whatever chat software a library is using should be accessible to all users, not just those with the latest hardware. Would you as a remote user care if your library were using the best, most up-to-date software if it would not work on your computer? Or would something simpler but less cutting edge be better if it could be used by all patrons without generating great levels of frustration?

Similarly, opportunities for displaying interest, listening, and following up abound in the virtual reference setting. The virtual librarian can repeat questions back to the user to display interest and make sure they are really hearing what the patron is communicating. As with face-to-face reference, one can follow up virtually by asking if the information provided met the patron's need and indicating that the remote user should contact the librarian again if they require additional assistance.

While 24/7 virtual chat reference may seem new and exciting, in many ways it is simply an extension of already existing forms of reference service. The introduction of telephone reference service was probably originally viewed with similar anticipation and apprehension. Users are remote in both situations, although chat technology allows some possibilities not available via the telephone. Librarians may actually push Web pages or do a step-by-step demonstration in chat reference, or they may send URLs, specific instructions, or lists of citations via e-mail. Whatever form reference service takes, it still consists of a librarian interacting with a patron whether the two can see one another or not. And with the increasing availability of Webcams in the virtual environment, this barrier may routinely cease to exist as well in virtual reference interactions.

These general common sense guidelines are very important in all reference transactions. In many instances, however, the patron has unique concerns or needs which call for us to transcend the standard behaviors discussed above. The reference librarian should be especially sensitive to spoken or unspoken feedback from the patron. Often there are subtle or obvious clues that can alert us to a patron's particular circumstances. Listen for statements such as:

- "This is the first time I've ever been in this library."
- "I've been here for three hours and haven't found a thing!"
- "I looked and this wasn't on the shelf where it should have been."
- "I have a research paper due in two days and just have to have this article!"
- "The librarian at the main library said this branch library was supposed to have the book I need, but I can't find it."

The empathetic librarian should be particularly alert to such clues. If you imagine yourself in the patron's position, you can understand the fear or frustration that lies behind some of these statements. At other times, the patron may not overtly voice such concerns. The savvy librarian must attempt to pick up on nonverbal clues to gain some understanding of the patron's situation or feelings. This may be particularly difficult in the virtual reference environment where nonverbal cues are absent. Emoticons or all caps may be the only clues to what the remote patron is truly feeling.

Such situations call for an extra dose of empathy and understanding. One should strive to understand what the patron is feeling. They may feel totally lost in the library or they may have severe time constraints, sometimes caused by their own procrastination, sometimes not. You should try not to judge, but instead put yourself in their place and consider what you would like in that situation. Maybe they did procrastinate, but would you really want a lecture from a stern librarian if you had a paper due tomorrow? Or would you welcome a librarian coming alongside you and doing their very best to assist you in your time of need?

Suppose you have never been in a specific library before, and you mention this fact to a librarian. You ask the librarian to direct you to the books on cloning, and they hastily jot down a call number, hand it to you, and cursorily wave their hand to indicate that the books are somewhere over that way. They don't even bother to walk you to the specific section you need. Is this how you personally would like to be treated if you were in totally unfamiliar surroundings and had said so to the librarian? Wouldn't you appreciate the librarian getting up and showing you the specific location of the item for which you are looking?

Or imagine the opposite, where a librarian is *too* helpful. You only have a few minutes on your lunch break to find the books by Mark Twain, and you mention this to the librarian. The librarian, instead of simply looking up the call number, has you sit down at a computer where they proceed to describe how to search for books by author, title, and subject, and how to find journal articles about Twain's writings. Such an example is obviously extreme, but it does illustrate how being insensitive to the patron's circumstances and pursuing one's own agenda as a librarian could negatively impact a reference encounter.

Extensive reference interviews and one-on-one instruction are obviously not bad or unimportant, but they are not always appropriate and can be taken to extremes. If the patron only wants one piece of information, don't try to teach them to use the whole library. They may only want to be shown where a particular item is located in the library and would become frustrated if made to sit down and learn all the nuances of searching the online catalog. Detailed instruction may have to wait for another day. Other patrons may desire to learn the nuances of how to search a database and use a thesaurus. If the patron appears receptive and provides positive feedback to your initial suggestion that you teach them how to conduct their own searches, then that is your green light to continue. The Golden Rule does not mean that we do a patron's work for them and abdicate all responsibility for teaching them how to use the library, but it does require that we be sensitive to their needs and desires at that moment. If they say they have class in five minutes, then by all means, lead them directly to the item on the shelf as quickly as possible. It all boils down to being sensitive to a patron's circumstances.

Remote users may also desire specific instruction so that they may replicate a search later on their own and become independent searchers. The opportunity to teach how to use the library and search efficiently still exists in the virtual reference setting. The concept of information literacy is not excluded from the virtual environment, although the empathetic librarian must still attempt to ascertain how open a remote patron is to this idea.

In the virtual reference environment, the librarian should also keep in mind what they as a patron would like if they were a remote user. Remote users typically do not want to be told to just come into the library for assistance although in some instances this may actually be appropriate or even necessary. Such users often prefer to do all of their work remotely and rely on online information sources such as the Web and e-journals. The very fact that they are using a virtual reference service indicates that they were not initially inclined or able to come to the library to do their research. Therefore, the virtual librarian should do all that is in their power to meet the needs of such users remotely. Only when absolutely necessary should they direct remote users to actually come to the library to use better information that is only available in that physical location.

Virtual reference also offers the opportunity to look beyond what the individual reference librarian can do in a single reference transaction and explore new services for the library as a whole. This might include expanded interlibrary loan and document delivery services to meet the special needs of remote users.

Some additional special considerations should be kept in mind regarding the Golden Rule. There are limits to its applicability especially if this involves inherently unethical behavior. The classic example is that of a masochist treating others how they would wish to be treated.[5] Because one likes to have pain inflicted upon oneself, this does not suggest that it would be right to inflict pain upon another. The Rule assumes that others want the same things we do, which may not always be true. What is implied is a kind of societal average concerning expected treatment. In a library setting, the Rule must also remain subject to federal and state laws as well as library policies. You do not look the other way because you would like a librarian to do so if you were a patron with criminal tendencies. Societal norms and laws still apply. However, if a patron does need reprimanding for a minor infraction of library rules, you should do so in a friendly, respectful manner.

As a professional librarian, you may rarely find yourself in the actual role of library patron standing at a reference desk. It may therefore be helpful to think of times when you have been served by another, perhaps by a store clerk, a server in a restaurant, or a doctor. What factors determined how successful you felt your interaction with that person had been? Thinking back on such situations may help you to picture yourself in the patron's place in a library setting. Just giving the patron the impression that you are trying to be empathetic and on their side can turn a potentially negative situation into a positive one.

So, the next time you're at the reference desk (physical or virtual) and someone approaches you, stop and think. Imagine you are the one on the other side of the desk. How would you like to be treated?

## NOTES

1. Miller, Bill. "Common Sense and the Golden Rule," *American Libraries* 30, no. 5 (1999): 60.

2. Rost, H.T.D. *The Golden Rule: A Universal Ethic.* Oxford: George Ronald, 1986.

3. Wattles, Jeffrey. *The Golden Rule.* New York: Oxford University Press, 1996, 3.

4. American Library Association. Reference and Adult Services Division. RASD Ad Hoc Committee on Behavioral Guidelines for Reference and Professional Services.

*Guidelines for Behavioral Performance of Reference and Information Services Professionals,* January 1996. Available online http://www.ala.org/Content/Navigation_Menu/RUSA/Professional_Tools4/Reference_Guidelines/Guidelines_for_Behavioral_Performance_of_Reference_and_Information_Services_ Professionals. Accessed 22 October 2002.

5. Wattles, *The Golden Rule,* 176-7.1

# Reference Services in Rural Libraries

Amanda E. Standerfer

**SUMMARY.** The information age has changed libraries of all types and sizes in ways that no one could have predicted. For a rural library, though, changes have been fast and furious and have made a dramatic impact on the very nature of the library and the services the library offers. Rural libraries went from a gathering place for community activities to fully wired information centers in a matter of a few years. The article addresses what these changes mean for reference services–one of the most basic functions of a public library. While people are consuming more information than ever, will the rural library be able to keep up with this demand even with the Internet? The article explores reference services in rural public libraries, using examples from libraries in central and northern Illinois, giving consideration to the nature of reference services, how they have changed over time, and how this compares to small libraries in a metropolitan setting. *[Article copies available for a fee from The Haworth Document Delivery Service: 1-800-HAWORTH. E-mail address: <docdelivery@haworthpress.com> Website: <http://www.HaworthPress.com> © 2006 by The Haworth Press, Inc. All rights reserved.]*

**KEYWORDS.** Rural public libraries, small public libraries, reference services, electronic resources, issues and trends, staff training, future of reference

---

Amanda E. Standerfer is Library Director, Helen Matthes Library, 100 East Market Avenue, Effingham, IL 62401-3499 (E-mail: amandas@effinghamlibrary.org).

[Haworth co-indexing entry note]: "Reference Services in Rural Libraries." Standerfer, Amanda E. Co-published simultaneously in *The Reference Librarian* (The Haworth Information Press, an imprint of The Haworth Press, Inc.) No. 93, 2006, pp. 137-149; and: *New Directions in Reference* (ed: Byron Anderson, and Paul T. Webb) The Haworth Information Press, an imprint of The Haworth Press, Inc., 2006, pp. 137-149. Single or multiple copies of this article are available for a fee from The Haworth Document Delivery Service [1-800-HAWORTH, 9:00 a.m. - 5:00 p.m. (EST). E-mail address: docdelivery@haworthpress.com].

## WHAT IS A RURAL LIBRARY?

The U.S. Census Bureau defines a rural place as one having fewer than 2,500 people. However, the Center for the Study of Rural Librarianship defines rural as a place with less than 25,000 people and is outside of a metropolitan area.[1] Both definitions of rural are worth looking at when considering public library services. Statistics from the U.S. Department of Education, National Center for Education Statistics show that 79 percent of the public libraries in the United States serve populations up to 25,000, and of those 29 percent serve populations up to 2,500.[2] While many of the 79 percent of public libraries may be in suburban areas, these statistics show that a large majority of the public libraries in the U.S. serve small communities, with almost a third serving rural communities as defined by the U.S. Census Bureau.

Illinois is a largely rural state with a large metropolitan and suburban area in Chicago and the surrounding collar-counties. Illinois had 646 public libraries serving 11.3 million state residents in 2001. The number of public libraries serving a population under 25,000 was 547 (85 percent), with 226 (35 percent) of those serving a population under 3,000.[3] In both cases, Illinois has a slightly higher number of small and rural libraries than the U.S. as a whole.

To focus more on reference services, though, this paper will look more specifically at the rural libraries in the Rolling Prairie Library System (RPLS), which is headquartered in Decatur, in central Illinois. In RPLS, of the fifty public libraries, forty-three (86 percent) of them serve a population under 25,000, with twenty (40 percent) of them serving a population under 2,500. The two large libraries in RPLS are in Springfield and Decatur, both serving populations between 80,000-115,000 people.[4]

To get an even more extensive picture of how reference services in these rural libraries stack up, this paper will also look at reference services in libraries serving similar populations in the North Suburban Library System (NSLS), headquartered in Wheeling, which consists of forty-nine public libraries in the north-west suburbs of Chicago. Only eighteen (37 percent) of these forty-nine libraries serve a population of less than 25,000, and none serve less than 2,500.[5] While these libraries are considered small libraries, rather than rural, since they are located near a larger metropolitan area, it is still useful to compare reference services in these libraries to gain a better understanding of the issues and trends that are impacting both.

Total operating income for rural RPLS libraries ranged from $11,000 to $722,000 in 2001. For most of these libraries, local property taxes are the main source of income, usually 70 percent or more. On the other hand, the total operating income for small NSLS libraries ranged from $110,000 to $2.5 million in 2001. For these NSLS libraries, though, local property taxes were generally 80 percent or more of their income.[6]

By 2001, all rural RPLS and small NSLS libraries had Internet access. Most libraries had Internet access for staff and patrons. For the RPLS libraries, a partially state-funded program called the Illinois Century Network brought high-speed Internet access to most rural libraries; however, some still rely on dial-up connections, though cable Internet and DSL are becoming more readily available. In 2001, only two NSLS libraries reported that their card catalog was not yet automated, compared to nine RPLS libraries.[7] The Internet provided many challenges to small and rural libraries because it brought the information age to many people who might not have had a lot of access to information in the past, especially in the rural areas.

To better understand reference services in rural public libraries in RPLS and small public libraries in NSLS, a survey was conducted. This survey asked a library staff member to respond to a series of questions about print and electronic reference resources in their library, about trends they have noticed in providing reference services over the past five years, and about their opinion of the future of reference services in their library. While the number of respondents to the survey was rather low (only eleven of forty-three libraries in RPLS and six of eighteen libraries in NSLS), the information gathered from these surveys is useful in drawing out some trends in the changes in reference services over the past five years. Responses and survey statistics are incorporated in the discussion below.[8]

## *WHAT DEFINES REFERENCE SERVICES?*

Reference services are often considered one of the primary functions of a public library and can be defined in many ways, but basically it is responding to requests for information by patrons. There are many ways, however, that a library can go about providing reference services. In a rural public library, reference services may be very limited for many reasons, for example, lack of trained personnel (sometimes lack of any personnel), lack of proper sources to answer the request, or lack of space for the proper reference sources.

Reference services are listed as one of the important programs and services that a rural public library should offer according to Linda Johnson's article, "The Rural Library: Programs, Services, and Community Networks." This article discusses the importance of partnering with other libraries or consortia to provide innovative reference services to meet the special information needs of the rural community that the library is serving.[9] However, the first half of the article is devoted to describing services that rural libraries can and do offer, including reference, but the second half describes the "model of service" found in the Beaumont (CA) Library District where reference services are not even mentioned. While undoubtedly this library offers some kind of reference services, it is interesting to note that the author chose to focus more on youth services, summer reading programs, humanities programs, etc., and not on reference services.

Johnson's article is typical of several books on the management and administration of small public libraries. Very little space is devoted to reference services and how to provide reference services. More attention, rather, is paid to customer service and sources to use when a patron does have a question. These books do not negate the fact that reference services should be provided by small libraries, they just do not give a lot of focus to practical approaches for providing reference services on a limited budget, with limited space, and limited staff training.[10]

This lack of emphasis on reference services is likely typical of many rural libraries: the libraries are there, but they are not significant enough to talk about for any length of time. More and more, rural public libraries are being spread thin by trying to offer more services to meet the needs of specialized population groups in their communities and by trying to "be all things to all people." Reference services seem to get lost in the shuffle; they are there, but it is not always evident.

In most of the rural RPLS libraries, reference services are very limited. Many of the responding libraries only have one to two employees, and both often work part-time. In these libraries, reference services are provided by whoever is at the circulation desk. In some of the larger rural libraries in RPLS (those serving over 9,000), reference services are a little more advanced. Most of these libraries have at least one part-time employee who is devoted to providing reference services. One of the libraries that responded to the survey indicated that they had just hired a full-time reference librarian with a master's in library and information science from an American Library Association accredited university. Another responding library indicated that they were in the process of getting a similar position approved. For both libraries, these positions had gone unfilled in the past, but an increasing demand for reference services made them necessary again.

In the smaller NSLS libraries, a similar variation in responses exists. The smaller NSLS libraries provide reference services on demand, and many do not even have a formal reference desk. However, the larger of the small NSLS libraries have one or more employees devoted to providing reference services. Demand and budget is one of the biggest differences between the RPLS and NSLS libraries. Most of the RPLS libraries indicated that there was not a demand for reference services, and even if there were, many of the libraries would not be able to afford to staff the service. On the other hand, because of a higher demand for reference services, the NSLS Libraries are able to afford staff devoted to reference.

## HOW HAS THE INFORMATION AGE IMPACTED REFERENCE SERVICES?

The Internet has brought reference services to a whole new level, though, and has acted as an equalizer between large and small public libraries, and even between small and rural public libraries. Before the predominance of the Internet and the availability of Internet computers in libraries, librarians in all sizes of libraries had to rely on print sources, back-up phone reference, or the occasional subscription to an electronic reference resource. In Illinois, the Illinois State Library provides select OCLC FirstSearch databases (some even full-text) to public libraries that are members of the regional library systems for no cost. This allows many rural libraries to offer more reference services than they did in the past.

Many of the rural RPLS libraries indicated that they had the same number or an increase in electronic resources (such as CD-ROMs and online databases) in the past five years. Most of these libraries, though, did not indicate an increase in spending on electronic resources. This is probably due to an increase in the number of electronic resource offerings the Illinois State Library provided during the previous year at no cost, including NoveList, a readers' advisory database. The state library is continuing to preview other resources.

The small NSLS libraries indicated that they definitely had an increase in the number of electronic resources and spending on these resources in the past five years. Their responses point more directly to the growing importance of CD-ROMs and online databases for reference

services in small suburban libraries. The amount spent on electronic resources was much higher than the RPLS libraries and the nature of the
comments made was much more favorable to the electronic resources
than the comments made by RPLS libraries. This difference, though, is
not surprising given the fact that most of the NSLS libraries provide a
higher level of reference service than the RPLS libraries, and given the
fact that the NSLS libraries' budgets are significantly higher than those
in RPLS.

### IS PRINT DEAD?

Comparing the expenditures on electronic resources to the expenditures on print reference volumes was quite different in the different areas of Illinois. The RPLS libraries were nearly evenly split on whether
or not their print reference collection had increased in the past five
years. A few libraries said that the size of their collection had remained
the same, but an even number reported an increase or a decrease, showing that some libraries were still building their print reference collections despite the availability of more no-cost electronic resources.
Spending on print reference materials varied widely with most of the
RPLS libraries, though, the spending on print reference materials has
decreased in the past five years.

Several of the rural RPLS libraries indicated that they were simply
not able to expand their print reference collections due to space constraints. One library indicated that the size of their reference collection
had to be decreased in order to make room for more popular collections,
in this case the large-print books. Another library indicated that they
were not replacing as many of their print reference sources now that
they had more electronic resources and access to the Internet. A third library said that they were decreasing the size of their entire non-fiction
collection to keep up with their patrons' demand for popular fiction.

The NSLS libraries indicated either a decrease or a stable number of
reference volumes in their collections, showing that most were not actively building their reference collections. These libraries may be just
replacing older reference sets for newer editions and not adding a lot of
new materials. The difference between the NSLS and RPLS libraries is
in the dollar amount of spending on print reference materials. Even five
years ago, some libraries reported spending as much as $67,000 on print
reference materials, and most said that that amount had either remained
the same or increased slightly. The libraries that reported high spending

on print reference materials have book budgets that are larger than the entire operating budgets of some of the rural RPLS libraries, but proportionally many of the small NSLS libraries spent more on print reference materials than the rural RPLS libraries. The smaller of the small libraries in NSLS, though, report a much lower amount spent on print reference materials, as low as $500, five years ago and now. The libraries that reported these low amounts are also the ones that indicated a lesser demand for reference services overall in their libraries. Only one of the small NSLS libraries indicated that their print reference collection was limited by space constraints. The other respondents to the survey mostly indicated that their print reference collections had decreased because of lack of demand for the print sources and more reliance on electronic reference sources.

## STAFF TRAINING ISSUES

Staff training is another issue for rural public libraries. The Internet may have brought more reference resources into the rural library, but are the staff members trained to provide access to that information? And even if the staff member can find the information, are they able to recall the information and pass it along to patrons when needed?

In almost all of the rural RPLS libraries, reference services are often provided by the staff member that is at the circulation desk at the time of the patron's request, and this staff member may or may not have any training on providing reference services. Three of the RPLS libraries indicated that they have staff (or are planning to have staff) devoted at least part-time to providing reference services. In one of those libraries, the staff member has a MLIS from an ALA-accredited institution, and in the other, the staff member has a bachelor's degree in an unrelated field. In the third library, they are hoping to hire a MLIS librarian to provide the reference services. In the smaller of the responding RPLS libraries, the education level of the staff ranges from a high school diploma to a bachelor's degree (in two libraries), with one library having a staff member with a Library Technical Assistant (LTA) certificate recently completed through a distance learning program.

For all of the RPLS libraries, continuing education about reference services was a problem. Most said that their staff had received no training on providing reference services in the past five years. A few of the libraries indicated that their staff had received training through in-house workshops, the regional library system (RPLS), the Illinois State Library, or the Illinois Library Association. Only two of the libraries said that a staff member had received formal college or university training on reference services in the past five years.

Most NSLS libraries indicated that their reference staff has received some training on reference services over the past five years. Lack of training was not a problem as it was for RPLS library staff members. Many of the libraries have MLIS degreed librarians providing reference services, but even the smaller libraries indicated that their staff had received training from either in-house workshops, the regional library system (mostly NSLS), the Illinois State Library, or the Illinois Library Association.

## THE FUTURE OF REFERENCE SERVICES IN THE SMALL AND RURAL PUBLIC LIBRARY

A recent survey of 655 rural libraries across the U.S. indicated that 92 percent of librarians use the Internet to answer reference questions.[11] Certainly, that statistic alone proves that the Internet has become the most important resource in rural libraries when providing reference services. The survey respondents for this article concur, whether they are in small suburban libraries or rural libraries.

### NSLS Respondents

For almost all of the small NSLS libraries, reference services are an important part of the total library service package. Reference services are gaining in importance and the way that they are provided is changing rapidly. One NSLS respondent indicated that his library is "always seeking ways to improve service." Several of the respondents indicated that a lot of patrons had already conducted a basic Internet search before coming to the reference desk, thus making it more important for the reference staff to be savvy on using multiple sources to come up with a complete answer for the patron. While most of the NSLS libraries said their print reference collections were declining, several said they still use some print reference sources because they are not able to find specific enough information from online resources.

Almost all of the NSLS respondents said something about the importance of the Internet and other electronic resources in providing reference services at their library. One respondent said that their library was "able to rely on the Internet, whether through free or subscription databases, for most of our reference questions, use of print sources has decreased." Another library indicated that they were doing a study of their print reference materials and they expected that they would do a lot of weeding as a result. For most of the NSLS libraries, reliance and use of print reference sources was declining. One respondent summed up what a lot of the NSLS small libraries must be feeling when she said, "You can't look at reference services with a five year plan. Changes occur much more rapidly than planning documents can be created. Be ready to implement change on a monthly basis."

## *RPLS Respondents*

For a majority of the rural RPLS libraries, reference services have become more important, but will probably continue to be a secondary service to children and young adult services and popular adult fiction. These libraries have seen a change in the amount of reference materials available to them through electronic resources, but have received little to no training on how to use these resources to answer reference questions in their libraries. With rural areas becoming more reliant on information for the advancement of their communities, it seems as if the local public library could step up and fill this role as the place citizens could access information. However, without the proper training on how to find, validate, and use electronic resources, library staff members may not be able to fill that community need.

For some of the larger rural RPLS libraries, reference services have already gained a larger role in the library. Three of the libraries that serve over 9,000 people indicated that reference service is a growing area in their libraries. In at least one of these libraries, the respondent indicated that reference questions "are more complex and represent the public's expectation that smaller libraries can now answer reference questions traditionally reserved for larger libraries." The response points to the Internet and the increased availability of electronic resources for this change. Another RPLS respondent said that there "seems to be a greater need for reference and that need is very broad in scope." This respondent also stated that she would like to see more regularly scheduled workshops on reference and perhaps even guidelines as to "what is considered quality reference depending on the size of the library."

Several of the RPLS respondents indicated that their reference services were more instructional than just answering questions or providing information. With more public access to Internet computers available in these rural libraries, patrons are relying on library staff members to show them how to use the computer. Anything from typing a letter to setting up an e-mail account on the Internet is being asked of library staff members. Staff skills must go beyond knowing how to find information to knowing how to use a computer and instruct others.

## WHAT DOES IT ALL MEAN FOR RURAL PUBLIC LIBRARIES?

Don Dillman's article, "Community Needs and the Rural Public Library," saw the emerging demand for information in rural America. The article states that "rural America has little choice but to get adequately connected to the nation's telecommunications systems so that its businesses can compete."[12] Twelve years later, with rural America wired, the impact on the rural public library has been staggering. Dillman stated that in 1991 "computer access needs to become a fundamental right in society."[13] Hopefully, rural libraries have stepped up to this challenge.

For the rural RPLS public libraries, especially the ones that serve populations over 9,000, the information age is constantly changing how reference services and information is provided to patrons. One respondent indicated that as more reliable Web sites become available, the more his library will reduce the number of volumes in their print reference collection. Several respondents talked about the importance of providing reference services to students, and how the information age has helped expand the amount and variety of information available in even the smallest, rural public library. One respondent said that students rely more and more on the public library for homework questions, "probably due to lack of school spending on libraries/librarians." Several respondents indicated that the nature of reference questions in their libraries was changing. One library said that questions are becoming more "technical," while another library said that they spend more time answering questions about how to "do things on the computer, like save a document to a disk." Another library indicated that the "ability to locate material quickly—especially full-text articles from periodicals has changed reference services."

While electronic resources, especially those available freely on the Internet, are changing the way rural libraries provide reference services, there is still a void in training library staff to find, validate, and use these resources. One RPLS respondent said, "As long as reference librarians can recognize legitimate web domains, such as edu, gov, etc., electronic reference will continue to grow in public libraries and make the print versions obsolete." While this is true, the respondents indicated that they had little to no training on reference services in the past five years.

Several of the RPLS libraries indicated electronic resources helped them provide reference services to students doing homework or research papers. One respondent said that students "don't realize that everything on the Internet is not necessarily true and up to date." How are staff members in the rural public library supposed to be able to recognize valid Web sites, and then recall these sites when a patron poses a reference question if they have never been trained on how to find the sites in the first place? Perhaps the rural library staff member spends time surfing the Internet and finds answers to patron's reference questions on their own. However, without proper training, how will reference staff know that the information is accurate, up-to-date, and that there are no other sources available to help answer the question? These issues might be holding back rural public libraries from becoming the main place that citizens go for information and answers to their questions.

With the small and sometimes dwindling budgets of rural public libraries, many are not able to purchase electronic resources beyond what the Illinois State Library provides at no cost. One of the RPLS respondents indicated that "electronic sites are still too expensive for libraries, making the print version the only alternative." However, half of the responding RPLS libraries indicated a decrease in the number of print volumes in their reference collections. So many of the rural libraries are providing reference services with fewer print reference sources and no-cost electronic resources.

A recent article concurs that the Internet has dramatically changed reference services in rural public libraries. The author says by putting print reference sources aside for Internet sources, libraries save "both money and space for other resources." The Internet has expanded the rural public library's reference collection "to all kinds of information that is not 'on-site.'"[14]

The bottom line, though, is that rural libraries are, to paraphrase Theodore Roosevelt, doing the best that they can, with what they have, where they are. One RPLS respondent said, "Most people don't really expect a small public library to be able to provide much in the way of reference services, and are surprised to find that we provide it." Even with little to no training, rural RPLS libraries, as is probably the case with many rural public libraries across the U.S., do their best to get the information that their patrons want and need. Luckily, this has become easier in the past five years with the availability of no-cost electronic resources, like those provided by the Illinois State Library and through the Internet. This trend will most likely continue, as rural public libraries decrease their spending on and space for reference collections, and increase their reliance on electronic resources. Hopefully, training opportunities for staff on how to find and use electronic resources will become more of a priority over the next five years.

## NOTES

1. Center for the Study of Rural Librarianship. *Profile of Rural Public Libraries in the United States.* Updated 15 August 2003. Available from Accessed 16 August 2003.

2. United States. Department of Education. National Center for Education Statistics. *Public Libraries in the United States: Fiscal Year 1999.* 2002.

3. Illinois State Library; University of Illinois at Urbana-Champaign, Library Research Center. *Illinois Public Library Statistics: A Guide for Librarians and Trustees,* 2000-01. Urbana, IL, 2000. Book online. Available from http://lrc.lis.uiuc.edu/IPLAR/FY2001/summary.pdf. Accessed 18 August 2003.

4. Ibid., http://lrc.lis.uiuc.edu/IPLAR/FY2001/tables/system/rpls/income.pdf. Accessed 31 August 2003.

5. Ibid., http://lrc.lis.uiuc.edu/IPLAR/FY2001/tables/system/nsls/income.pdf. Accessed 31 August 2003.

6. Ibid., or http://lrc.lis.uiuc.edu/IPLAR/FY2001/tables/system/nsls/income.pdf. Accessed 31 August 2003.

7. Ibid., or http://lrc.lis.uiuc.edu/IPLAR/FY2001/tables/system/rpls/automat.pdf. Accessed 31 August 2003.

8. Libraries that responded from NSLS: Glencoe Public Library; Lake Bluff Public Library; McHenry-Nunda Public Library District; Morton Grove Public Library; Prospect Heights Public Library District; and Winnetka-Northfield Public Library District. Libraries that responded from RPLS: Athens Municipal Library; Chatham Area Library District; Helen Matthes Library, Effingham; Greenup Township Public Library; Lincoln Public Library District; Maroa Public Library District; Mason City Public Library District; Carnegie-Schuyler Public Library, Pana; Pawnee Public Library; Stonington Public Library; and Barclay Public Library District, Warrensburg.

9. Johnson, Linda. The Rural Library: Programs, Services, and Community Coalitions and Networks. *Rural Libraries* 20, 2 (2000): 48-49.

10. See Sager, Donald J. *Small Libraries: Organization and Operation.* Fort Atkinson, WI: Highsmith Press, 2000. Reed, Sally Gardner. *Small Libraries: A Handbook for Successful Management.* Jefferson, NC: McFarland & Co., Inc., 2002. Weingand, Darlene E. *Administration of the Small Public Library.* Chicago: American Library Association, 2001.

11. Flatley, Robert. Rural Librarians and the Internet: A Survey of Usage, Attitudes, and Impact. *Rural Libraries* 21, 1 (2001): 9.

12. Dillman, Don. Community Needs and the Rural Public Library. *Wilson Library Bulletin* 65, 9 (1991): 32.

13. Ibid., 155.

14. Heuertz, Linda, Andrew C. Gordon, and Margaret T Gordon. The Impact of Public Access Computing on Rural and Small Town Libraries. *Rural Libraries* 23, 1 (2003): 63.

# Index

Those numbers followed by t indicate a table.

# BOOK ORDER FORM!

Order a copy of this book with this form or online at:
http://www.haworthpress.com/store/product.asp?sku= 5727

## New Directions in Reference

___ in softbound at $19.95 ISBN-13: 978-0-7890-3089-4 / ISBN-10: 0-7890-3089-6.

___ in hardbound at $34.95 ISBN-13: 978-0-7890-3088-7 / ISBN-10: 0-7890-3088-8.

---

**COST OF BOOKS** _____

**POSTAGE & HANDLING** _____
US: $4.00 for first book & $1.50
for each additional book.
Outside US: $5.00 for first book
& $2.00 for each additional book.

**SUBTOTAL** _____
In Canada: add 7% GST. _____

**STATE TAX** _____
CA, IL, IN, MN, NJ, NY, OH, PA & SD residents
please add appropriate local sales tax.

**FINAL TOTAL** _____
If paying in Canadian funds, convert
using the current exchange rate,
UNESCO coupons welcome.

❑**BILL ME LATER:**
Bill-me option is good on US/Canada/
Mexico orders only; not good to jobbers,
wholesalers, or subscription agencies.

❑**Signature** _____

**Payment Enclosed: $** _____

❑ **PLEASE CHARGE TO MY CREDIT CARD:**

❑Visa ❑MasterCard ❑AmEx ❑Discover
❑Diner's Club ❑Eurocard ❑JCB

**Account #**_____

**Exp Date** _____

**Signature** _____
(Prices in US dollars and subject to change without notice.)

---

### PLEASE PRINT ALL INFORMATION OR ATTACH YOUR BUSINESS CARD

Name

Address

City     State/Province     Zip/Postal Code

Country

Tel     Fax

---

May we use your e-mail address for confirmations and other types of information? ❑Yes ❑No We appreciate receiving
your e-mail address. Haworth would like to e-mail special discount offers to you, as a preferred customer.
**We will never share, rent, or exchange your e-mail address.** We regard such actions as an invasion of your privacy.

Order from your **local bookstore** or directly from
**The Haworth Press, Inc.** 10 Alice Street, Binghamton, New York 13904-1580 • USA
Call our toll-free number (1-800-429-6784) / Outside US/Canada: (607) 722-5857
Fax: 1-800-895-0582 / Outside US/Canada: (607) 771-0012
E-mail your order to us: orders@haworthpress.com

**For orders outside US and Canada,** you may wish to order through your local
sales representative, distributor, or bookseller.
For information, see http://haworthpress.com/distributors

(Discounts are available for individual orders in US and Canada only, not booksellers/distributors.)

**Please photocopy this form for your personal use.**
www.HaworthPress.com

BOF06